Analysis of Sampled Imaging Systems

TUTORIAL TEXTS SERIES

- *Infrared Optics and Zoom Lenses,* Allen Mann, Vol. TT42
- *Introduction to Adaptive Optics,* Robert K. Tyson, Vol. TT41
- *Fractal and Wavelet Image Compression Techniques,* Stephen Welstead, Vol. TT40
- *Analysis of Sampled Imaging Systems,* R. H. Vollmerhausen and R. G. Driggers, Vol. TT39
- *Tissue Optics: Light Scattering Methods and Instruments for Medical Diagnosis*, Valery Tuchin, Vol. TT38
- *Fundamentos de Electro-Óptica para Ingenieros,* Glenn D. Boreman, translated by Javier Alda, Vol. TT37
- *Infrared Design Examples,* William L. Wolfe, Vol. TT36
- *Sensor and Data Fusion Concepts and Applications, Second Edition*, L. A. Klein, Vol. TT35
- *Practical Applications of Infrared Thermal Sensing and Imaging Equipment, Second Edition,* Herbert Kaplan, Vol. TT34
- *Fundamentals of Machine Vision,* Harley R. Myler, Vol. TT33
- *Design and Mounting of Prisms and Small Mirrors in Optical Instruments*, Paul R. Yoder, Jr., Vol. TT32
- *Basic Electro-Optics for Electrical Engineers,* Glenn D. Boreman, Vol. TT31
- *Optical Engineering Fundamentals,* Bruce H. Walker, Vol. TT30
- *Introduction to Radiometry,* William L. Wolfe, Vol. TT29
- *Lithography Process Control,* Harry J. Levinson, Vol. TT28
- *An Introduction to Interpretation of Graphic Images,* Sergey Ablameyko, Vol. TT27
- *Thermal Infrared Characterization of Ground Targets and Backgrounds,* P. Jacobs, Vol. TT26
- *Introduction to Imaging Spectrometers,* William L. Wolfe, Vol. TT25
- *Introduction to Infrared System Design,* William L. Wolfe, Vol. TT24
- *Introduction to Computer-based Imaging Systems,* D. Sinha, E. R. Dougherty, Vol. TT23
- *Optical Communication Receiver Design,* Stephen B. Alexander, Vol. TT22
- *Mounting Lenses in Optical Instruments,* Paul R. Yoder, Jr., Vol. TT21
- *Optical Design Fundamentals for Infrared Systems,* Max J. Riedl, Vol. TT20
- *An Introduction to Real-Time Imaging,* Edward R. Dougherty, Phillip A. Laplante, Vol. TT19
- *Introduction to Wavefront Sensors,* Joseph M. Geary, Vol. TT18
- *Integration of Lasers and Fiber Optics into Robotic Systems,* Janusz A. Marszalec, Elzbieta A. Marszalec, Vol. TT17
- *An Introduction to Nonlinear Image Processing,* E. R. Dougherty, J. Astola, Vol. TT16
- *Introduction to Optical Testing,* Joseph M. Geary, Vol. TT15
- *Image Formation in Low-Voltage Scanning Electron Microscopy,* L. Reimer, Vol. TT12
- *Diazonaphthoquinone-based Resists,* Ralph Dammel, Vol. TT11
- *Infrared Window and Dome Materials,* Daniel C. Harris, Vol. TT10
- *An Introduction to Morphological Image Processing,* Edward R. Dougherty, Vol. TT9
- *An Introduction to Optics in Computers,* Henri H. Arsenault, Yunlong Sheng, Vol. TT8
- *Digital Image Compression Techniques,* Majid Rabbani, Paul W. Jones, Vol. TT7
- *Aberration Theory Made Simple,* Virendra N. Mahajan, Vol. TT6
- *Single-Frequency Semiconductor Lasers,* Jens Buus, Vol. TT5
- *An Introduction to Biological and Artificial Neural Networks for Pattern Recognition,* Steven K. Rogers, Matthew Kabrisky, Vol. TT4
- *Laser Beam Propagation in the Atmosphere,* Hugo Weichel, Vol. TT3
- *Infrared Fiber Optics,* Paul Klocek, George H. Sigel, Jr., Vol. TT2
- *Spectrally Selective Surfaces for Heating and Cooling Applications,* C. G. Granqvist, Vol. TT1

Analysis of Sampled Imaging Systems

Richard H. Vollmerhausen
Ronald G. Driggers

Tutorial Texts in Optical Engineering
Volume TT39

Donald C. O'Shea, Series Editor
Georgia Institute of Technology

SPIE PRESS
A Publication of SPIE—The International Society for Optical Engineering
Bellingham, Washington USA

Library of Congress Cataloging-in-Publication Data

Vollmerhausen, Richard H.
    Analysis of sampled imaging systems / Richard H. Vollmerhausen and Ronald G. Driggers
      p. cm. – (Tutorial texts in optical engineering ; v. TT39)
    Includes bibliographical references and index.
    ISBN 0-8194-3489-2 (softcover)
    1. Imaging systems—Image quality. 2. Image processing—Statistical methods. 3. Fourier
    analysis. 4. Sampling (Statistics) I. Driggers, Ronald G. II. Title. III. Series.
TK8315.V65 2000
621.36'7—dc21   99-058678
                                                          CIP

Published by

SPIE—The International Society for Optical Engineering
P.O. Box 10
Bellingham, Washington 98227-0010
Phone: 360/676-3290
Fax: 360/647-1445
Email: spie@spie.org
WWW: www.spie.org

Printed in the United States of America.

INTRODUCTION TO THE SERIES

The Tutorial Texts series was begun in response to requests for copies of SPIE short course notes by those who were not able to attend a course. By policy the notes are the property of the instructors and are not available for sale. Since short course notes are intended only to guide the discussion, supplement the presentation, and relieve the lecturer of generating complicated graphics on the spot, they cannot substitute for a text. As one who has evaluated many sets of course notes for possible use in this series, I have found that material unsupported by the lecture is not very useful. The notes provide more frustration than illumination.

What the Tutorial Texts series does is to fill in the gaps, establish the continuity, and clarify the arguments that can only be glimpsed in the notes. When topics are evaluated for this series, the paramount concern in determining whether to proceed with the project is whether it effectively addresses the basic concepts of the topic. Each manuscript is reviewed at the initial state when the material is in the form of notes and then later at the final draft. Always, the text is evaluated to ensure that it presents sufficient theory to build a basic understanding and then uses this understanding to give the reader a practical working knowledge of the topic. References are included as an essential part of each text for the reader requiring more in-depth study.

One advantage of the Tutorial Texts series is our ability to cover new fields as they are developing. In fields such as sensor fusion, morphological image processing, and digital compression techniques, the textbooks on these topics were limited or unavailable. Since 1989 the Tutorial Texts have provided an introduction to those seeking to understand these and other equally exciting technologies. We have expanded the series beyond topics covered by the short course program to encompass contributions from experts in their field who can write with authority and clarity at an introductory level. The emphasis is always on the tutorial nature of the text. It is my hope that over the next few years there will be as many additional titles with the quality and breadth of the first ten years.

Donald C. O'Shea
Georgia Institute of Technology

CONTENTS

Preface   xi

1   **Introduction / 1**
    1.1   Description of a sampled imager / 2
    1.2   Description of the sampling process / 4
    1.3   Linearity and shift invariance / 7
    1.4   Signal reconstruction / 12
    1.5   Three ways of viewing the sampling process / 14
            1.5.1   The displayed image is the sum of its parts / 14
            1.5.2   The display is a filter of the image samples / 17
            1.5.3   The display is a filter of the sampled image / 19

2   **Fourier integral representation of an optical image / 23**
    2.1   Linear, shift-invariant optical systems / 23
    2.2   Spatial and frequency domain filters / 26
    2.3   Reducing LSI imager analysis to one dimension / 28
    2.4   The MTF associated with typical imager components / 31
            2.4.1   Optical filtering / 32
            2.4.2   Detector spatial filters / 34
            2.4.3   Electronic filtering / 36
            2.4.4   Display filtering / 36
            2.4.5   Filtering by the human eye / 38
    2.5   Temporal filters / 40

3   **Sampled imager response function / 45**
    3.1   Fourier transform of a sampled image / 46
    3.2   Derivation of the sampled imager response function / 52
    3.3   Examples of sampled imager response functions / 54
            3.3.1   Example 1: The pictures of Lena in Chapter 1 / 55
            3.3.2   Example 2: Effect of changing sample rate / 56
            3.3.3   Example 3: Midwave infrared sensor / 65
    3.4   Definition and calculation of the spurious response ratio / 68

4   **Sampled imager design and optimization / 73**
    4.1   Interpolation and image reconstruction / 73
    4.2   Classical design criteria for sampled imaging systems / 84

4.3   Minimum resolvable temperature difference, miminum
        resolvable contrast, and the half-sample limit / 88
4.4   MTF Squeeze / 92
4.5   Sampled imager optimization / 95
        4.5.1   Gaussian pre-sample blur and Gaussian post-sample
                  blur / 96
        4.5.2   Gaussian pre-sample blur and rectangular post-sample
                  blur / 101
        4.5.3   Optimizing the display of a 256 by 256 staring array
                  imager / 105

5   Interlace and dither / 111
5.1   Sampling improvement with static scene / 114
5.2   Resolution and sensitivity / 119
5.3   Effect of scene to sensor motion / 122

**6   Dynamic sampling, resolution enhancement, and super
         resolution / 125**
*Contributed by Jonathon M. Schuler and Dean A. Scribner, Optical
Sciences Division, U.S. Naval Research Laboratory*
6.1   Introduction / 125
6.2   Sampling limitations of the focal plane array topology / 126
        6.2.1   Review of discrete image sampling / 126
        6.2.2   The fundamental limitation of the FPA sampling / 127
6.3   Dynamic sampling / 130
6.4   Ambient optical flow as a novel sampling mechanism / 130
        6.4.1   Shift estimation / 130
        6.4.2   Generalized motion estimation / 134
6.5   Image restoration / 136
6.6   Conclusion / 137

7   The Sampling Theorem / 139
7.1   Theory / 139
7.2   Example / 141
7.3   Discussion / 143

**8   Laboratory measurements of sampled infrared imaging system
         performance / 147**
8.1   Classical infrared imager performance measurements / 148
        8.1.1   Sensitivity / 148
        8.1.2   Resolution / 150
        8.1.3   Human performance – minimum resolvable temperature
                  difference / 152
8.2   Sampled infrared imager performance measurements / 153

      8.2.1   Sensitivity / 156

      8.2.2   Resolution – modulation transfer function / 159

      8.2.3   Human performance - minimum resolvable temperature difference / 161

Appendix A: Fourier series and Fourier integrals / 165

      A.1 Fourier series / 165

      A.2 Fourier integral / 167

Appendix B: The impulse function / 171

      B.1 Definition / 171

      B.2 Properties of the impulse function / 171

Index / 173

PREFACE

This tutorial is written for the design engineer or system analyst who is interested in quantifying the effect of sampling on imager performance. It is assumed that the reader has at least some background in linear systems and Fourier transform methods. However, a review of these subjects is included in Chapter 2 and the appendices.

Sampled imagers are not new, and optimizing the design of sampled imagers is not a new topic. Television imagery has always been vertically sampled, for example. From its inception as a mechanically scanned Nipkow disk, television imagery consisted of a raster of horizontal lines. Television raster effects were analyzed by Otto Shade (*Perception of Displayed Information*, ed. Biberman, 1973) and many others. Over the years, these analysts developed "rules of thumb" for minimizing raster effects and optimizing the viewed image. Television manufacturers have undoubtedly developed their own proprietary design rules. Whatever the analytical or experiential basis, designers have done an outstanding job of minimizing visible raster and other sampling artifacts in commercial television.

However, advancing technology in solid state detector arrays, flat panel displays, and digital image processing has led to a greatly increased variety of sampled imaging products and possibilities. These technology developments provide new opportunities and problems for the design engineer and system analyst.

An extensive variety of InSb and PtSi mid-wave focal plane arrays has been developed in the last few years, and this trend continues with HgCdTe, quantum wells, and thermal focal plane detectors. A common characteristic of the imagers that use these focal planes is that they are undersampled. The typical InSb imager circa 1998 uses a 256×256 detector array and the best available array is 512×512 or 640×480. The relatively sparse sample spacing provided by these detector arrays can lead to artifacts which degrade the displayed imagery.

Poor sampling can corrupt the image by generating localized disturbances or artifacts. The corruption will result in shifting object points, lines and edges. Poor sampling can also modify the apparent width of an object or make a small object or detail disappear. That is, a fence post imaged by an undersampled sensor can be seen as thicker, thinner, or slightly misplaced.

Although larger, better-sampled arrays are under development, we expect that the lower resolution arrays will be used in many systems for years to come. In addition to good availability, the low resolution arrays are cheaper, smaller, and require less electronic processing hardware. Further, in many applications, multispectral or color imagery is more useful than high-resolution imagery, and it is often necessary to sacrifice high resolution in order to achieve a multispectral or color capability.

The cost and difficulty of displaying high-resolution imagery is also a significant design consideration. While the cathode ray tube (CRT) is still the preeminent choice for display quality, flat panel displays have size and form-factor advantages that can override other considerations. However, flat panel displays lack both the addressability and Gaussian blur characteristics that make the CRT such a flexible and desirable display medium. Flat panel displays can have sharply demarcated pixels (that is, pixels with sharply defined edges), and the pixels are at fixed, uniformly spaced locations in the display area. These flat panel characteristics can lead to serious sampling artifacts in the displayed image.

Images on flat panel displays can exhibit artifacts such as blocky representations of objects, stair-stepping in lines and arcs, jagged edges, and luminance gaps or bands. A CRT image can exhibit visible raster lines. These display artifacts make it difficult for the human visual system to spatially integrate the underlying image. These artifacts do not arise from corruption of the baseband image by aliasing; these artifacts arise from the display characteristics.

The quality of a sampled image depends as much on the display technique as on the number of samples taken by the sensor. While the display cannot overcome the fundamental limitations of the sensor, sensor information is often hidden by a poor display choice.

In this text, Fourier transform theory is used to describe and quantify sampling artifacts like display raster, blocky images, and the loss or alteration of image detail due to aliasing. The theory is then used to predict the type and level of sampling artifacts expected for a particular sensor and display combination. Knowing the sensor and display design, the various kinds of sampling artifacts are predictable and can be quantified using the analytical technique described in this book.

This book also provides metrics (that is, the design rules) that can be used to optimize the design of a sampled imager. In practical systems, control of sampling artifacts often entails increased pre-sample or post-sample filtering. Increased pre-sample filtering can be accomplished by defocusing the objective lens, for example, and increased post-sample filtering can be accomplished by defocusing the CRT display spot. This increased filtering can help performance by removing sampling artifacts but degrades performance by blurring the displayed image. We present methods that can be used to quantify these sampled-imager design trade-offs.

There are a number of excellent texts on the application of Fourier transform theory to imaging systems including *Linear Systems, Fourier Transforms, and Optics* (Wiley) by J. Gaskill and *Fourier Optics* (McGraw-Hill) by J. Goodman. These texts discuss ideal sampling and the Sampling Theorem, but they do not address either the sampling artifacts found in practical sensors or sampled system design optimization. This book addresses the application of Fourier theory to practical, sampled systems.

One important topic not covered in this book is the existence of the Fourier transform when dealing with physical systems. For an excellent discussion of this topic, we cannot do better than refer the reader to the preface and first two chapters of Bracewell's *The Fourier Transform and Its Applications* (McGraw-Hill, 1986).

In this book, it is assumed that the spatial and temporal functions associated with real (realizable, physical) systems have a Fourier transform. In some cases, the Fourier transform cannot be found by directly evaluating the Fourier integral as described in Chapter 2 of this book. This happens, for example, when the function to be integrated is periodic and does not decrease to zero as frequency approaches infinity. These functions are not absolutely convergent to zero and the Fourier integral cannot be evaluated.

It turns out, however, that the ability to evaluate the Fourier integral is a sufficient, but not necessary, condition for the existence of the Fourier transform. Mathematical "tricks" can be used to discover the Fourier transform even when the integral does not exist.

We assume that all functions of physical interest have a Fourier transform. As stated by Bracewell on pages 8 and 9 of *The Fourier Transform and Its Applications*:

> *A circuit expert finds it obvious that every waveform has a spectrum, and the antenna designer is confident that every antenna has a radiation pattern. It sometimes comes as a surprise to those whose aquaintance with Fourier transforms is through physical experience rather than mathematics that there are some functions without Fourier transforms. Nevertheless, we may be confident that no one can generate a waveform without a spectrum or construct an antenna without a radiation pattern....The question of the existence of transforms may be safely ignored when the function to be transformed is an accurately specified description of a physical quantity. Physical possibility is a valid sufficient condition for the existence of a transform.*

Sampling theory and sampled imager analysis techniques are covered in Chapters 1 through 4. Chapter 1 introduces several subjects important to the discussion of sampled imagers.

Chapter 2 describes the Fourier representation of the imaging process. Fourier electro-optics theory relies on the principle of linear superposition. An imager is characterized by its response to a point of light. The image of a scene is the sum of the responses to the individual points of light constituting the original scene. The Fourier transform of the blur spot produced by the optics (and detector and other parts of the imaging system) when imaging a point of light is called the Optical Transfer Function (OTF). The amplitude of the OTF is the Modulation Transfer Function, or MTF. Experience has shown that MTF is a good way to characterize the quality of an imaging system. An image cannot be defined until the scene is described, but the characterization of the imager's response to a point source provides a good indication of the quality of images which can be expected under a variety of environments.

In Chapter 3, Fourier theory is extended to sampled imaging systems. A response function for sampled imagers is derived by examining the image formed on the display by a point source of light in the scene. The response of a sampled system to a point source depends on sample phase; that is, the response depends on the distance between the point source and a sample location. It is true, therefore, that the image expected from a sampled imager cannot be defined without first specifying the scene. However, the response function is a good way to characterize both the quality of the sampled imager and its tendency to generate sampling artifacts.

The design of sampled imaging systems is discussed in Chapter 4. First, the effect of interpolation on display quality is described. Next, the optimization of sampled imaging systems is performed using a number of classical design guidelines. Finally, a new optimization technique, the MTF squeeze, is described, and optimization using this technique is compared to the classical techniques.

Chapter 5 describes interlace and dither. Interlace and dither (dither is sometimes called microscanning) improve sensor sampling without increasing detector count. A high-resolution frame image is comprised of two or more lower-resolution field sub-images taken in time sequence. Between each field sub-image, a nodding mirror or other mechanical means is used to move the locations where the scene is sampled. Interlace and dither achieve high resolution while minimizing focal plane array complexity. Chapter 5 describes the sampling benefits of interlace and dither, and also discusses the display artifacts which can arise when scene-to-sensor motion occurs.

Dynamic sampling is covered in Chapter 6. This chapter was contributed by Jonathon Schuler and Dean Scribner of the Naval Research Laboratory. With high-performance computers and digital processors, resolution enhancement is now possible by combining multiple frames of an undersampled imager to construct a well-sampled image. First, the optical flow of the image is computed to determine the placement of the samples. "Super-resolution" can then be achieved by combining the dynamic sampling techniques with an image restoration process.

Chapter 7 is devoted to the Sampling Theorem. The Sampling Theorem is described and an example given of a near-ideal reconstruction of a sampled waveform. The primary purpose of the chapter, however, is to discuss the limited value of the Sampling Theorem in evaluating real systems. The Sampling Theorem assumes that the signal is band-limited before sampling and that an ideal filter is used to reconstruct the signal. In practical systems, neither criteria is met. The Sampling Theorem does not provide a basis for evaluating real systems since it is the compromises to the rules of the Sampling Theorem that are the essence of practical system design.

The techniques and problems associated with the measurement of sampled imaging system performance are presented in Chapter 8. Sampled imaging systems are not shift-invariant, and the output imagery contains spurious response artifacts. Measurements on these systems require special procedures.

Finally, the appendices provide a summary of the Fourier integrals and series along with the characteristics of impulse functions. These two appendices are intended to be reference sources for the mathematics described in the main text.

Richard H. Vollmerhausen
Ronald G. Driggers
February 2000

Analysis of Sampled
Imaging Systems

1

INTRODUCTION

This chapter provides an introduction to several topics.

First, the physical processes involved in sampling and displaying an image are discussed. In a staring sensor, the image is blurred by the optics, and then the detector array both blurs and samples the image. The detector samples are then used to construct the displayed picture. Those physical processes that occur in a sampled imager are described.

It is convenient when analyzing sampled systems, however, to conceptually separate the pre-blur, sampling, and post-blur (display blur) attributes of the system. These three steps in the generic sampling process are described and the importance of each step discussed.

Next, the system properties known as *linearity* and *shift invariance* are discussed. Systems which are both linear and shift invariant can be characterized by a transfer function. Circuits and optical systems, for example, can be characterized by their Modulation Transfer Functions (MTF). This chapter describes the transfer function concept using an electrical, low-pass filter as an example. For linear, shift-invariant systems, the transfer function provides a quantitative way of characterizing system behavior.

Sampled systems are linear, so Fourier transform theory can be used to analyze sampled systems. However, sampled systems are not shift invariant. It is the lack of the shift invariance property which differentiates sampled systems from other systems and makes sampled systems more difficult to analyze. The lack of shift invariance in a sampled system is illustrated. Also, the reasons that a sampled system cannot be assigned a transfer function are explained.

At the end of this chapter, three different mathematical ways of representing the sampling processes are presented. These three derivations correspond to three different physical views of the sampling process. The physical basis of the mathematical techniques used in Chapter 3 is described, and the role of the display in a sampled system is put into perspective.

For simplicity, many of the examples in this chapter are one-dimensional, but the discussion and conclusions apply to two-dimensional imagery.

1.1 DESCRIPTION OF A SAMPLED IMAGER

Figure 1.1 shows a camera imaging a scene and an observer viewing the sampled image on a display.

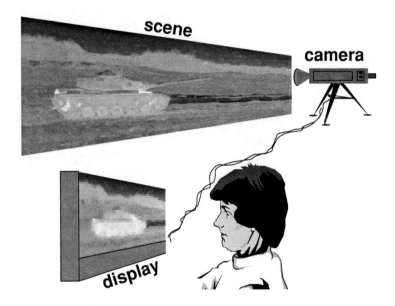

Figure 1.1 Observer viewing the display of a sampled image.

The components of the camera are shown in Figure 1.2. A lens images the scene onto a staring detector focal plane array (FPA). Diffraction and aberrations in the optics result in blurring the image presented to the FPA. In the figure, the image on the FPA is upside-down as well as blurred, because the optical system inverts the image.

The detector array consists of a number of rows and columns of individual detectors as shown in the inset in Figure 1.2. Photo-detection occurs over the active area of these individual detectors; that is, the incoming light generates photo-electrons. Since each detector integrates photo-signal over a finite active area, the detector itself also blurs the image. Individual points in the optical image are summed together if they fall on the same detector, and this summing of adjacent points causes a blur.

The individual detector photo-current is integrated (in a capacitor, charge well, or by some other mechanism) for a period of time. Periodically, generally every sixtieth of a second in the United States or every fiftieth of a second in Europe, the resulting signal charge is read-out, and the integrator is reset. The amount of charge from each detector depends directly on the intensity of light falling on that detector. The charge output from each detector represents a sample of the lens- and detector-blurred scene intensity.

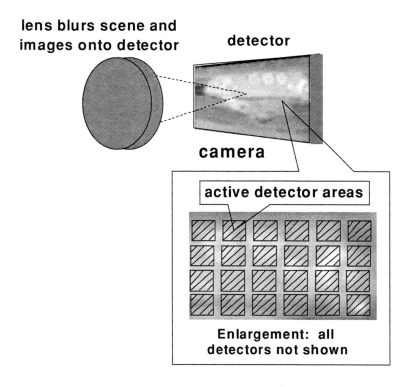

Figure 1.2 Components of camera shown in Figure 1.1. Lens images scene onto detector array. Optical diffraction and aberrations in lens blur the image. The detector further blurs image by integrating signal over active detector area. Each detector provides one sample of the blurred scene.

Note that, in the example shown in Figure 1.2, the active detector area does not cover the whole FPA. This array does not have a 100% fill factor.

The two images in Figure 1.3 summarize the action of the camera. Conceptually, the optical and detector blurs are lumped together and called the pre-sample blur. The image with optical and detector pre-sample blur applied is shown in the left-hand picture in Figure 1.3. The detectors then convert the light intensity at specific locations in the blurred image to electrical signals. The electrical signals represent image samples. In the right-hand picture, the white dots indicate the locations where the blurred image is sampled by the detector array.

A display device is used to *reconstruct* the image from the detector (electrical) samples. The display device consists of an array of individual display pixels. A "display pixel" is an individual, light-emitting area on the display surface. In the simplest case, the number and location of pixels in the display correspond to the number and location of detectors in the FPA. The brightness of each display pixel is proportional to the photo-signal from the corresponding detector.

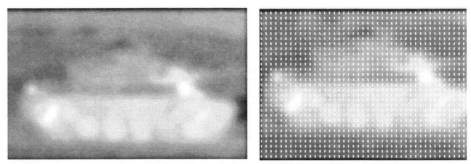

Figure 1.3 Left-hand picture shows image blurred by optics and detector. Right-hand image shows location of detector samples as white dots.

Figure 1.4 shows the display. An individual display pixel is shown in the upper, left-hand corner of the image. These pixels happen to be square. In this example, there is one display pixel for each sensor sample shown in Figure 1.3. The intensity of each pixel shown in Figure 1.4 is proportional to the photo-intensity at the corresponding sample location in Figure 1.3.

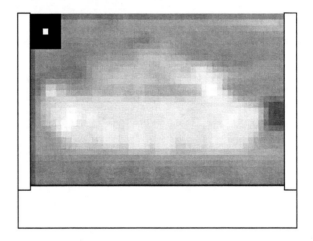

Figure 1.4 Display of sampled image. An individual pixel is shown at upper, left-hand corner. Each pixel on the display is illuminated in proportion to the amplitude of the sample from the corresponding location in Figure 1.3.

1.2 DESCRIPTION OF THE SAMPLING PROCESS

Sampled imaging systems can be characterized by a three-step process. First, the original image of Lena shown in Figure 1.5(a) is degraded by a pre-sample blur. The blur is caused by the combined effects of optical diffraction and aberrations, the finite size and shape of the detector, camera vibration, motion smear, and other effects. The pre-sample, blurred image is shown in Figure 1.5(b). Next, the blurred image is sampled; that is, some, generally electronic, mechanism is used to find the amplitude of the blurred image at discrete points. In this example, the blurred image in Figure 1.5(b) is sampled at the points shown as white dots in Figure 1.5(c). The third step is reconstruction of the image. Each sensor sample controls the intensity of a display pixel (or a group of display pixels). This is *zoom* shown in Figure 1.5(d). The shape and size (intensity distribution) of the display pixels determines the post-sample blur. The shape and size of an individual display pixel is shown at the upper, left-hand corner of Figure 1.5(d). The post-sample blur (reconstruction blur) also includes any post-sampling electronic filtering and eye blur.

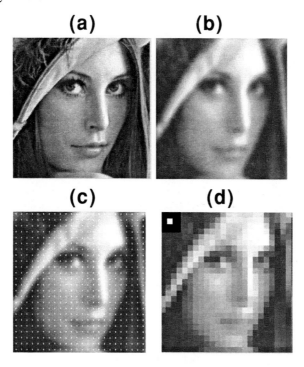

Figure 1.5 Original picture in (a). Pre-sample blur applied to original in (b). Picture (c) shows locations of samples. Picture (d) shows reconstructed image. A single display pixel is shown in the upper, left-hand corner of picture (d).

All three stages of the sampling process are necessary: pre-blur of the image, sampling, and post-blur or reconstruction. Figure 1.6(a) shows the result of sampling the original image without pre-filtering [that is, Figure 1.5(a) is sampled rather than Figure 1.5(b)]. In this case, aliasing hurts the final, displayed image. Figure 1.5(d) looks more like Figure 1.5(a) than Figure 1.6(a) does.

Figure 1.6(b) shows the image samples displayed as points rather than the large pixels used in Figure 1.5(d). In Figure 1.6(b), the image is not blurred by the display pixel, and the image cannot be integrated by the eye. To get a good image, display reconstruction using a post-sample blur is necessary.

As an illustration, move Figure 1.6(b) close to the eye so that only points are seen. Now, move the figure slowly away from the eye. Lena begins to appear as the figure moves away because eye blur acts as a reconstruction filter.

(a)   (b)

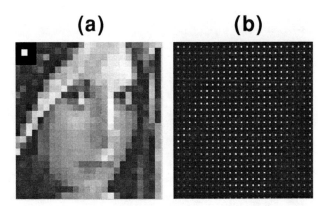

Figure 1.6 The picture in (a) shows original image in Figure 1.5(a) sampled without pre-blur and then reconstructed in a similar manner to 1.5d. Figure 1.5(d) looks more like Figure 1.5(a) than Figure 1.6(a) does; some pre-sample blurring is necessary. The picture in (b) is constructed with pixels which are spatially much smaller than the pixel pitch: The pixels in (b) do not blur the image, and the picture is very hard for the eye to integrate. Post-blur of the image samples is necessary.

Rules can be established for determining the optimum relationship between pre-blur, sample spacing, and post-blur. A well-sampled imaging system is one where the spacing (in milliradians or millimeters) between image samples is small compared to the width of the pre-sample blur. In this case, sampling artifacts are not apparent in the image.

An undersampled imaging system is one where the sample spacing is a large fraction of the pre-sample blur. Depending on scene content, the artifacts caused by under-sampling can limit the performance of the imaging system. Poor sampling can corrupt the image by generating localized disturbances or artifacts. The corruption results in shifting object points, lines and edges. Poor sampling can also modify the apparent width of an object or make a small object or detail disappear. That is, a fence post imaged by an undersampled sensor can be seen as thicker, thinner, or slightly misplaced.

An optimum post-blur depends on the sample spacing and other factors. If the display pixel is large compared to the sample spacing, then the image will be blurred. If the display pixel is small compared to the sample spacing, then the shape of the pixel itself might be visible. Display pixels which are individually visible because of their size or intensity distribution will add spurious content to the image. The spurious response due to poor image reconstruction can seriously degrade sensor system utility.

Visible raster or a "pixelated" display makes it difficult for the observer to integrate the underlying sensor imagery. This is certainly true for the picture in Figure 1.6(b), for example. However, the picture shown in Figure 1.5(d) is also degraded by the sharply demarcated display pixels. The picture of Lena in Figure 1.7 was generated using the same samples as used to generate the picture in Figure 1.5(d). The second picture is better because the display pixel shape provides a better match to the original image between sample points.

Figure 1.7 Picture of Lena reconstructed using the same samples as in Figure 1.5(d). This picture is better because the display pixel shape provides a better match to the original image between sample points.

A well-designed system is the result of a trade-off between sample rate or spacing, pre-sample blur, and display reconstruction. Too much pre-blur can limit performance by degrading resolution while wasting detector count. Too little pre-blur can cause significant aliased content that limits sensor performance. A display blur which is too small can introduce spurious responses like visible raster and pixelation effects that can ruin the displayed image. A display blur which is too large will limit performance by degrading resolution. Achieving good performance with a sampled imager requires trade-offs between the pre- and post-sample blurs and the sample spacing.

1.3 LINEARITY AND SHIFT INVARIANCE

Systems which are both linear and shift-invariant (LSI systems) can be analyzed in a very special way. A transfer function (or system response function) can be defined for an LSI system, where the transfer function completely describes system behavior. For example, most circuits have a transfer response function which describes their electrical behavior. A well-corrected optical telescope has an Optical Transfer Function which characterizes the image. LSI analysis is so common, and the ability to find a single function that completely describes a system is so typical, that it is ingrained in the modern engineering psyche. This section describes LSI theory and explains why it does not apply to sampled systems.

Systems are *linear* if superposition holds. That is, if:

input A yields ⇒ output A

and

input B yields ⇒ output B

then

input A + input B yields ⇒ output A + output B.

Sampled systems are linear.

Some linear systems are *shift invariant*. *Shift invariance* means that, if

input(t) yields ⇒ output(t)

then

input(t-τ) yields ⇒ output(t-τ).

In this example, t is time and τ is a fixed time offset. Shift invariance means that if an input is delayed τ seconds then the output is delayed τ seconds, but the shape of the output depends only on the shape of the input and does not change with the time delay. Sampled systems are not shift invariant. Note that the concept described here can be applied to space and spatial offsets. In that case, t and τ can be replaced by x and x_o.

Another feature of LSI systems is that the output of an LSI system contains only the same frequencies as were input. This also is not true for sampled systems.

A simple resistor-capacitor (RC) low-pass filter circuit is shown at the top of Figure 1.8. An input sinusoid and the resulting output are shown at the bottom of Figure 1.8. This circuit is both linear and shift invariant. The output sine wave is the same frequency as the input sine wave. If two sine waves are input, the output will be the sum of the individual outputs. If the input sine wave is delayed τ seconds, then the output sine wave is delayed by τ seconds.

In Figure 1.9, the output of the low-pass filter is sampled. The output is reconstructed using a sample and hold circuit. That is, the sample value is held constant for the entire sample period. At the bottom of Figure 1.9, the sampled output is shown along with the input and the pre-sampled output. (Note that the sampled output is shown shifted back in time, to the left, by one half of a sample period. In reality, the sampled output would be delayed [moved to the right in the figure] one half of a sample period. The sampled output is shown shifted back in time in order to show how its shape matches the pre-sample output.)

The sampled output shown in Figure 1.9 is not a sine wave at the same frequency as the input. The irregularly shaped output contains many different frequencies. Also, the sampled system is not shift invariant As illustrated in Figure 1.10, as the input moves in time, the position of the samples on the input

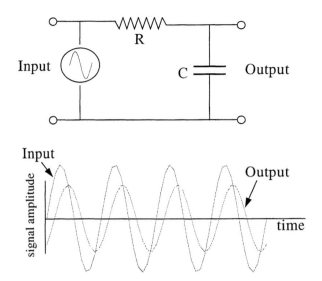

Figure 1.8 A low pass filter is an example of a linear, shift-invariant circuit. Output is at the same frequency as the input, and if input shifts in time, then the output shifts in time by the same amount without changing shape or amplitude.

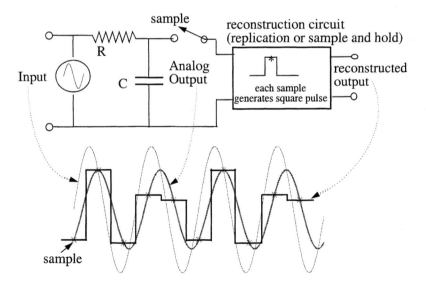

Figure 1.9 Low pass filter circuit with Sample and Hold on output. Output waveform has many frequencies which are not in the input spectrum.

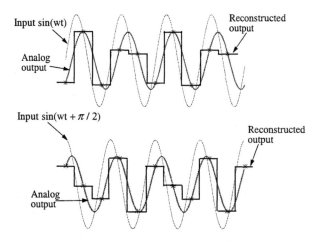

Figure 1.10 Waveform on top is sampled and reconstructed. At bottom, same waveform is shifted and then sampled and reconstructed. The output waveforms on top and bottom have different shapes. Sampling is not shift-invariant. The shape of the reconstructed output changes depending on the phase (the timing) of the input.

waveform changes. The shape of the sampled output changes depending on how the samples line up with the input. The shape of the sampled output depends on when the input occurs. The sampled system is not shift invariant.

A system function can be defined for a system which is both linear and shift invariant. A sinusoidal steady-state analysis completely defines the response of an LSI system. The response of an LSI system is defined by the relationship between the amplitudes A and B and the angles α and β for the system driving (forcing) function dr and response (output) function re:

$$dr(t) = A \cos(\omega t + \alpha) \tag{1.1}$$

$$re(t) = B \cos(\omega t + \beta) \tag{1.2}$$

where ω is 2π times frequency in Hertz.

If an LSI system is driven by a sinusoid, then the output will be a sinusoid at the same frequency, but the output will generally have a different amplitude and phase. Furthermore, if the relationship between the amplitude and phase of $dr(t)$ and $re(t)$ can be found for every angular frequency ω, then that relationship completely describes both the periodic and aperiodic responses of the system.

Using complex notation, with j representing the square root of minus one, the following functions represent the Fourier transforms of the driving and response functions.

$$Dr(\omega) = A(\omega)e^{j\alpha(\omega)} \tag{1.3}$$

$$Re(\omega) = B(\omega)e^{j\beta(\omega)} . \tag{1.4}$$

The transforms of the driving and response functions are related to each other by the system transfer function $H(\omega)$,

$$Dr(\omega) \;=\; H(\omega)\,Re(\omega) \tag{1.5}$$

where $H(\omega)$ is a complex function of the real variable ω. The system transfer function $H(\omega)$ completely characterizes the LSI system. Given an input $in(t)$, the output $o(t)$ is predictable from the equation:

$$O(\omega) \;=\; H(\omega)\,In(\omega) \tag{1.6}$$

where $In(\omega)$ and $O(\omega)$ are the Fourier transforms of the input and output, respectively.

The sinusoidal steady-state analysis described by Equations 1.1 through 1.6 is widely used in electrical circuit analysis and Fourier optics. For example, this analysis applies to the low-pass filter shown in Figure 1.8. Given an input $In(\omega)$, the output $O(\omega)$ is described by:

$$O(\omega) = \frac{1}{1+ j\omega RC}\,In(\omega) \tag{1.7}$$

Another term used to describe LSI systems is *constant parameter*. A system which can be described by a linear differential equation which has constant coefficients will always be linear and shift invariant. For example, the low-pass filter is described by the following differential equation:

$$\frac{Q}{C}+R\frac{dQ}{dt} = in(t) \tag{1.8}$$

or alternately:

$$\frac{1}{C}\int idt + iR = in(t) \tag{1.9}$$

where Q is charge, and i is current. In this example, both the resistance R and the capacitance C are constant (so the circuit has constant parameters), and the circuit is LSI.

Unfortunately, this kind of steady-state analysis does not apply to sampled systems. As shown by the Figure 1.9 example, a sine wave input to a sampled system does not produce a sine wave output at the same frequency. The frequency content of the output depends on the reconstruction method and the number of samples taken. Further, as shown in Figure 1.10, sampled systems are not shift invariant. The output depends on the relative position (or sample phase) of the samples compared to the input signal.

A transfer function like $H(\omega)$ in Equation 1.5 or 1.6 cannot be defined for a sampled system. However, as shown in the following chapters, a substitute for the system transfer response can be found for use with sampled systems.

1.4 SIGNAL RECONSTRUCTION

The degree to which a sampled output matches the original, pre-sample signal depends on the signal reconstruction technique as well as on the sample rate.

Figure 1.9 shows a sine wave reconstructed using a sample and hold. The sampled output is created by centering a rectangular pulse at each sample location. Each rectangular pulse is the width of a sample period, and the height of the pulse is the sample value. This type of signal reconstruction is called *replicated* because the sample value is used over and over.

Compare the sampled output in Figure 1.9 to the sampled output in Figure 1.11. In Figure 1.11, linear interpolation is used. Each sample is connected by a straight line. The sample rate has not changed, but the output generated using linear interpolation appears to be a better representation of the input.

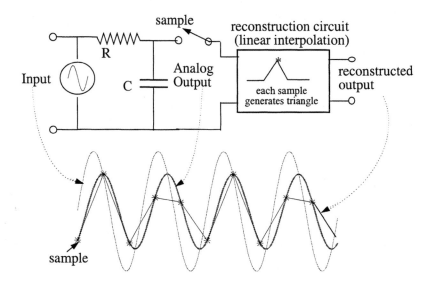

Figure 1.11 Low pass filter circuit sampled at same locations as in Figure 1.9. In this figure, the output is reconstructed by linear interpolation. That is, the samples are connected with straight lines. The sampled output in this figure matches the pre-sampled waveform better than the sampled output in Figure 1.9. Linear interpolation reconstructs the sampled waveform better than sample replication.

In order to make the subsequent example clearer, consider another way of implementing linear interpolation. This can be accomplished by centering a triangular pulse at each sample location. The pulse height is equal to the sample value, and the triangular half-width is equal to a sample period. Since adjacent triangles overlap, all triangle values at each time location are summed.

Now compare Figure 1.12 to Figures 1.9 and 1.11; the sampled output in Figure 1.12 is a much closer approximation to the pre-sampled signal. Again, the sample rate has not changed; the improvement derives from the reconstruction function used. In this case, the reconstruction function is a sinc wave [that is, a $\sin(x)/(x)$] multiplied by a Gaussian function. The reconstruction function shown in the box in Figure 1.12 is centered at each sample location. The amplitude at each sample location is equal to the sample value at that location. The sampled output is generated by summing the overlapping reconstruction functions at all times.

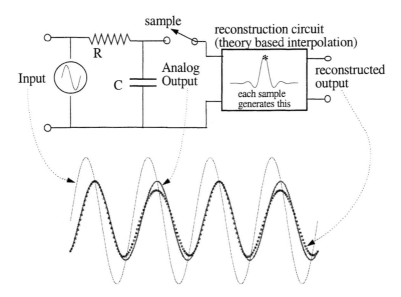

Figure 1.12 Low pass filter circuit sampled at same locations as in Figure 1.9. In this figure, the output is reconstructed by theory based (band-limited) interpolation. The sampled output in this figure matches the pre-sampled waveform better than the sampled output in Figures 1.9 or 1.11. Band-limited interpolation is better than either linear interpolation or replication.

The sampled output in Figure 1.12 is a better representation of the pre-sampled signal than the sampled output in Figure 1.9. The difference between the sampled outputs derives from the reconstruction technique, not the sample rate. The reconstruction function used in Figure 1.12 provides a better approximation of the original signal between the samples.

Once the samples are taken, other information about the pre-sampled signal is lost. However, if we know that the pre-sampled signal was essentially band-limited, then using replication to interpolate between samples cannot be correct; the resulting signal is certainly not band-limited. Knowing something about the pre-sampled signal, a better interpolation function can be generated, and the fidelity of the sampled output can be improved.

The quantitative benefit of improved interpolation techniques is described in future chapters. For the present, the reader is asked to consider two concepts. First, although the sample rate is an important factor in determining the fidelity of a sampled process, it is only one factor. The method used to reconstruct the signal (that is, the method used to interpolate between sample values) is also very important. Second, in most practical circumstances, nothing is known about the pre-sample signal except the samples themselves, but much is known about the pre-sample filtering. In Figure 1.12, for example, the characteristics of the low-pass filter are known. For images, the characteristics of the optical and detector components of the camera are known. Knowledge of the pre-sample filtering can be used to predict the value of the pre-sample signal between samples, thereby improving the fidelity of the output.

1.5 THREE WAYS OF VIEWING THE SAMPLING PROCESS

This section describes three different physical views of the sampling process. The three views each provide a different insight into the effects of sampling on imager performance. The mathematical derivations associated with each physical view quantify how the pre-sample (sensor) blur, the sample rate, and the post-sample (display) blur all affect the displayed image.

1.5.1 The displayed image is the sum of its parts

A sampled image is made up of individual display pixels, each illuminated in proportion to the focal plane array detector sample located at a corresponding spatial location. The image can be mathematically described as the sum of the individual pixels.

In Figure 1.13, the function $f(x)$ is sampled at uniformly spaced intervals. If N samples are taken with spacing X, an approximation $g(x)$ to $f(x)$ can be constructed:

$$g(x) = \sum_{n=0}^{N-1} f(nX)r(x-nX) \tag{1.10}$$

where $r(x)$, the reconstruction function, represents the intensity distribution (or shape and size) of an individual display pixel. Figure 1.14 shows the function $f(x)$, the reconstructed output $g(x)$, and the rect function used as $r(x)$ to generate the $g(x)$ shown. The selection of reconstruction function $r(x)$ and the sample interval X are fundamental to the fidelity with which $g(x)$ approximates $f(x)$. Different functions for $r(x)$, or a smaller spacing X, would lead to different functions $g(x)$ which better approximate $f(x)$.

Equation 1.10 shows that $g(x)$ is just the sum of the pixel shapes, each placed at its proper location in space and each weighted by the corresponding sample value.

The Fourier transform of $g(x)$ is $G(\xi)$, where ξ is the frequency in cycles per milliradian or cycles per millimeter. In the following expression, $F(\xi)$ is the Fourier transform of $f(x)$ and $R(\xi)$ is the transform of $r(x)$. $R(\xi)$ is the MTF for the intensity pattern associated with an individual display pixel. The Fourier transform of $r(x-nX)$ (that is, the Fourier transform for a display pixel located at location nX) is $R(\xi)\exp^{-j2\pi\xi nX}$. Therefore:

$$G(\xi) = \sum_{n=0}^{N-1} f(nX)R(\xi)e^{-j2\pi\xi nX}.\tag{1.11}$$

not function of x

Each display pixel is placed at the proper location and its intensity is weighted by the corresponding sample value. The Fourier transform $G(\xi)$ is just the sum of the transforms of the individual display pixels.

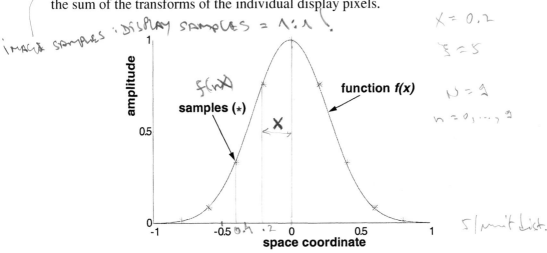

IMAGE SAMPLES : DISPLAY SAMPLES = 1:1 !

X = 0.2
ξ = 5
N = 9
n = 0, ..., 9

f(nX)

5/unit list.

Figure 1.13 The spatial function $f(x)$ is sampled at the points shown by asterisk (∗).

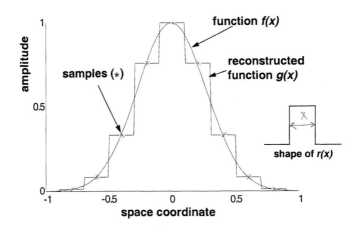

Figure 1.14 The function $f(x)$ is sampled at the asterisk (∗). The sample spacing is 5 per distance unit. The reconstructed function $g(x)$ is formed by placing a reconstruction function $r(x)$ at each sample location with a height equal to the sample value.

Figure 1.15 shows the Fourier transforms of the space domain functions $f(x)$ and $r(x)$; in this example, $f(x)$ is Gaussian and $r(x)$ is a rect function. Figure 1.16 shows the Fourier transform $G(\xi)$ of $g(x)$. Notice that, due to the sampling and reconstruction with a rect function, $G(\xi)$ contains frequencies not in $F(\xi)$.

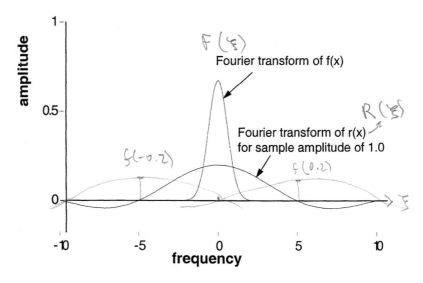

Figure 1.15 Fourier transforms $F(\xi)$ of $f(x)$ and $R(\xi)$ of $r(x)$. The function $f(x)$ is Gaussian and $r(x)$ is a rect function. The Fourier transform shown for $r(x)$ is for a unit amplitude rect function.

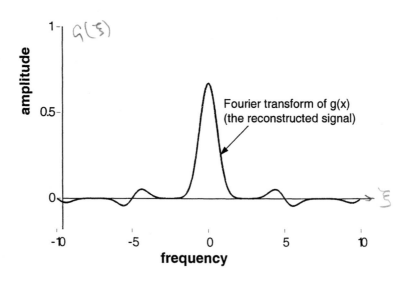

Figure 1.16 The Fourier transform $G(\xi)$ of $g(x)$. Notice that $G(\xi)$ contains frequencies not in $F(\xi)$. The sample rate is 5/(unit distance).

Equation 1.11 illustrates why a system transfer function cannot be assigned to a sampled system. In Equation 1.11, $R(\xi)$ is not acting to weight or filter the input spectrum $F(\xi)$; that is, $G(\xi)$ does not equal $F(\xi)R(\xi)$. $G(\xi)$ is a sum of $R(\xi)$ terms, not a product of $F(\xi)$ times $R(\xi)$. Further, frequencies not in $F(\xi)$ can exist in the output if they exist in $R(\xi)$.

The above derivations illustrate that the sampled output is just a sum of reconstruction functions, and the shape of the reconstruction function is fundamental in establishing the fidelity of the reconstructed signal. The samples control the frequencies in the output only by weighting the $\exp^{-j2\pi\xi nX}$ phase terms. Frequencies in $R(\xi)$ can be canceled or enhanced by the action of the weighted phase terms.

Equation 1.11 is the easiest and most straightforward way of obtaining the Fourier transform of a sampled image. Other analysis techniques, however, provide more insight into the relationship between the display, the sensor samples, and the pre-sample blur.

1.5.2 The display is a filter of the image samples

$S(\xi) = F\left\{ f(x) \cdot \sum_n \delta(x - nX) \right\}$

Equation 1.11 can be factored as shown in Equation 1.12.

$$G(\xi) = R(\xi)[\sum_{n=0}^{N-1} f(nX)e^{-j2\pi\xi nX}] \qquad (1.12)$$

Let:

$$S(\xi) = [\sum_{n=0}^{N-1} f(nX)e^{-j2\pi\xi nX}]. \qquad (1.13)$$

Now, $R(\xi)$ is a function of frequency that multiplies $S(\xi)$ (the function of frequency and X in the brackets). Figure 1.17 shows $S(\xi)$, $R(\xi)$ and the product $G(\xi)$; $G(\xi)$ is, of course, the same function as shown in Figure 1.16.

$S(\xi)$ is a periodic function of frequency which can be thought of as representing the Fourier transform of the samples of $f(x)$. The display MTF, $R(\xi)$, acts upon $S(\xi)$ to produce the displayed image.

In this view of the sampling process, an array of delta functions spaced X distance apart sample the intensity distribution $f(x)$. After sampling, the delta functions are viewed as a "bed of nails;" that is, the delta functions are very bright, very small points of light at the sample locations on the display. The integrated intensity of each point of light is equal to the image intensity at that location. The display pixel shape blurs these points of light to create the final, displayed image.

The delta functions are pulses with vanishingly small width and height such that the area under the delta function is one. Multiplying $f(x)$ by a delta function at location nX produces a delta function with area $f(nX)$.

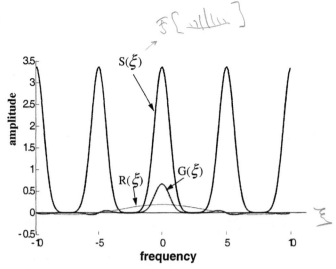

Figure 1.17 Figure shows the same $R(\xi)$ as in Figure 1.15 and the same $G(\xi)$ as in Figure 1.16. The amplitude (ordinate) scale has changed between these figures. $S(\xi)$, the Fourier transform of the "samples," is also shown in this figure. $G(\xi)$ results from multiplying $S(\xi)$ by $R(\xi)$.

This is true because the height of the delta function is scaled by the value of the intensity distribution at each location. Since the area under each delta function pulse is unity before the multiplication, the area of the product is the sample value.

Since the Fourier transform of a delta function of amplitude $f(nX)$ at location nX is $f(nX)\exp^{-j2\pi\xi nX}$, Equation 1.13 can be viewed as the Fourier transform of the samples of the $f(x)$.

Equation 1.12 can be derived using delta functions in the following manner.

$$g(x) = \sum_{n=0}^{N-1} f(x)\delta(x-nX) * r(x) \tag{1.14}$$

where (*) denotes convolution.

By the nature of the delta function,

$$f(x)\delta(x-nX) = f(nX)\delta(x-nX) \tag{1.15}$$

so that

$$g(x) = \sum_{n=0}^{N-1} f(nX)\delta(x-nX) * r(x). \tag{1.16}$$

A convolution in the space domain is a multiplication in the frequency domain. Taking the Fourier transform of both sides of Equation 1.16, and knowing that the Fourier transform of $\delta(x-nX)$ is $\exp^{-j2\pi\xi nX}$, Equation 1.12 gives the Fourier transform for $G(\xi)$.

Thus far, the sampling process has been dealt with in a physical and, hopefully, intuitive manner. However, Equations 1.12 and 1.16 have a limited utility in system analysis because they require the sample values. Also, the relationship between the pre- and post-sample blurs and the sample rate and phase is not explicit in Equation 1.12 and 1.16.

1.5.3 The display is a filter of the sampled image

A different, and more useful, expression for the Fourier transform can be found by starting with Equation 1.14. The new expression for $G(\xi)$ does not involve the sample values.

In all of the above sampling examples, the $x = 0$ origin is the first sample point. The function $f(x)$ is defined as the intensity distribution starting at the origin. The function $f(x)$ is simply whatever spatial distribution is being sampled. The above expressions for $g(x)$ and $G(\xi)$ do not lack generality because, in those expressions, $f(x)$ is only known by its sample values. If the imaged scene shifts, then $f(x)$ is re-defined, and new sample values are obtained at $f(nX)$, $n = 0, 1, 2,...$ N-1.

In the next view of the sampling process described below, we want to explore the behavior of $g(x)$ and $G(\xi)$ as the sample phase varies. The function $f(x)$ is a specific function in image space. The samples of $f(x)$ can be taken anywhere in space. As sample phase or position varies, the function $f(x)$ does not change, just where it is sampled.

Equation 1.14 is re-written to explicitly permit the function $f(x)$ to be located anywhere in sample space. This is done by letting $f(x)$ be offset in space by a distance x'. The origin at $x = 0$ is still a sample point.

$$g(x) = \sum_{n=0}^{N-1} f(x - x')\delta(x - nX) * r(x). \tag{1.17}$$

The Fourier transform is taken before the delta functions multiply $f(x)$. Since a multiplication in the space domain is a convolution in the frequency domain:

$$G(\xi) = [\sum_{n=0}^{N-1} F(\xi)e^{-j2\pi\xi x'} * e^{-j2\pi\xi nX}]R(\xi) \tag{1.18}$$

where (*) denotes convolution. In Equation 1.17 for the space domain, the function $f(x)$ multiplies the delta functions and the products are convolved with the reconstruction function $r(x)$. In Equation 1.18 for the frequency domain, the spatial products become frequency convolutions and the spatial convolutions become frequency products.

Equation 1.18 provides a general expression for $G(\xi)$ based on $F(\xi)$, $R(\xi)$, the sample spacing X, and the offset x'. However, this equation involves a messy convolution.

In order to simplify Equation 1.18, all space is sampled. The answer from sampling all space will equal the answer from sampling a finite interval only if $f(x)$ is zero outside the sampled interval. In the expression for $G(\xi)$ below, $F(\xi)$ is the Fourier transform of $f(x)$ limited to the sampled interval. That is, in the following, the Fourier transform of an image, $F(\xi)$, is the transform of the sampled part of the image.

This distinction is only important if $f(x)$ is thought to represent a whole scene, only part of which is sampled. In the derivation below, $f(x)$ must represent only the sampled part of the scene, and $F(\xi)$ is the Fourier transfer of that limited (windowed) $f(x)$.

If all space is sampled, then:

$$g(x) = \sum_{n=-\infty}^{\infty} f(x-x')\delta(x-nX) * r(x).$$

(1.19)

The Fourier transform of an infinite set of Dirac delta functions spaced X apart in the spatial domain is an infinite set of Dirac delta functions spaced $1/X$ apart in the frequency domain.

$$\Im[\sum_{n=-\infty}^{\infty} \delta(x-nX)] = \sum_{n=-\infty}^{\infty} \delta(\xi-n/X)$$

where   (1.20)

$\Im[] \equiv$ Fourier transform operation.

Therefore:

$$G(\xi) = [\sum_{n=-\infty}^{\infty} F(\xi)e^{-j2\pi\xi x'} * \delta(\xi - n/X)]R(\xi)$$

$$G(\xi) = R(\xi)\sum_{n=-\infty}^{\infty} F(\xi-n\nu)e^{-j2\pi(\xi-n\nu)x'}$$

$$G(\xi) = R(\xi)e^{-j2\pi\xi x'}\sum_{n=-\infty}^{\infty} F(\xi-n\nu)e^{j2\pi n\nu x'}$$

(1.21)

where

$$\nu = \frac{1}{X}.$$

The phase term $e^{-j2\pi\xi x'}$ represents a translation in space of the entire imaging process by a distance x'. This phase term can be ignored with no loss of information about the sampled system. The $e^{-j2\pi n\nu x'}$ term can be simplified. Let x'/X = integer M plus remainder d/X where $0 \le d \le X$. Also, remember that ν is $1/X$ (the sample spacing).

The output spectrum is

$f(x) \cdot \sum_n \delta(x - nX) \to$ sampled function

$\Rightarrow F(\xi) * \sum_n \delta\left(\xi - \frac{n}{X}\right)$ spectrum

$$G(\xi) = R(\xi) \sum_{n=-\infty}^{\infty} F(\xi - n\nu)e^{j2\pi n\nu x'}$$

$$G(\xi) = R(\xi) \sum_{n=-\infty}^{\infty} F(\xi - n\nu)e^{jn2\pi x'/X}$$

$$G(\xi) = R(\xi) \sum_{n=-\infty}^{\infty} F(\xi - n\nu)e^{jn2\pi M}e^{jn2\pi d/X}$$

$$G(\xi) = R(\xi) \sum_{n=-\infty}^{\infty} F(\xi - n\nu)e^{jn2\pi d/X} \tag{1.22}$$

$$G(\xi) = R(\xi) \sum_{n=-\infty}^{\infty} F(\xi - n\nu)e^{jn\phi}$$

where

$\phi \equiv$ sample phase in radians.

This view of the sampling process is illustrated in Figure 1.18. The pre-sample image spectrum is replicated at every integer multiple of the sample frequency. This is shown in Figure 1.18(a). Also shown in Figure 1.18(a) is the display MTF. The Fourier transform of the image is found by multiplying the replicated spectrum by the display MTF. The resulting image spectrum is shown in Figure 1.18(b).

The phase of each adjacent replica changes by the sample phase. If the display MTF does not filter out the replicas of $F(\xi)$ adjacent to the baseband, then the displayed image will vary with sample phase.

Equation 1.22 relates the displayed image spectrum to the spectrum of the pre-sampled function, the sample spacing, the sample phase, and the display MTF. Equation 1.22 quantitatively describes the relationship between the various stages of the sampling process. This equation allows us to explore design tradeoffs in a sampled imager.

BIBLIOGRAPHY

Bracewell, R. N., *The Fourier Transform and Its Applications*, McGraw-Hill, New York, NY, 1986.

Gaskill, J., *Linear Systems, Fourier Transforms and Optics,* Wiley: New York, NY, 1978.

Goodman, J. W., *Introduction to Fourier Optics,* McGraw-Hill: San Francisco, CA, 1968.

Holst, G. C., *Sampling, Aliasing, and Data Fidelity,* SPIE Optical Engineering Press, Bellingham, WA, 1998.

LePage, W. R., *Complex Variables and the Laplace Transform for Engineers*, Dover Publications, Inc, New York, NY, 1961.

Oppenheim A. V. and R. W. Schafer, *Digital Signal Processing,* Prentice-Hall: Englewood Cliffs, NJ, 1975.

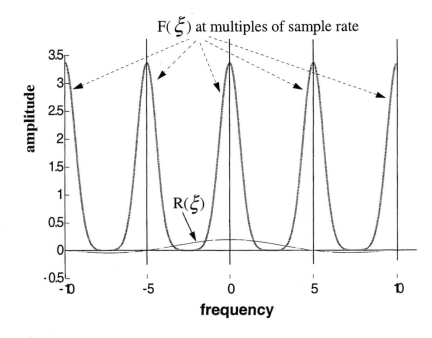

Figure 1.18(a) Sampling replicates the spectrum $F(\xi)$ at every integer multiple of the sample frequency. In this case, the sample rate is 5 per unit distance. The MTF of the display, $R(\xi)$, then multiplies the replicated spectra. The result is the image spectrum $G(\xi)$ shown in the next figure.

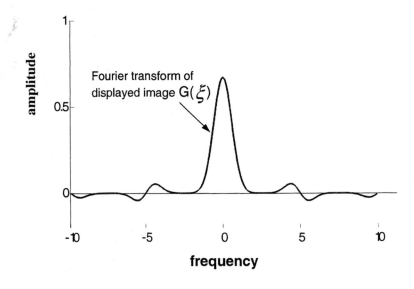

Figure 1.18(b) The Fourier transform of the displayed image $G(\xi)$ obtained by multiplying replicas of $F(\xi)$ at each multiple of the sample rate by the display MTF $R(\xi)$. This $G(\xi)$ shown here and in Figure 1.16 are the same.

2

FOURIER INTEGRAL REPRESENTATION OF AN OPTICAL IMAGE

2.1 LINEAR, SHIFT-INVARIANT OPTICAL SYSTEMS

In Figure 2.1, a simple optical system is imaging a clock onto a screen. For simplicity, unity magnification is assumed (that is, the image is the same size as the object). As illustrated in the lower left corner of the image, each point source in the object becomes a *point spread function* (*psf*) in the image. The point spread function is also called the *impulse response* of the system. Each point in the scene is blurred by the optics and projected onto the screen. This process is repeated for each of the infinite number of points in the scene. The image is the sum of all the individual blurs.

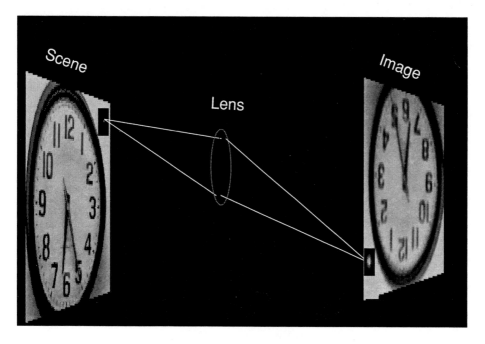

Figure 2.1 Clock being imaged by a lens onto a screen; a point source in the scene (upper right) becomes a point spread function blur in the image (lower left).

Two considerations are important here. First, the process of the lens imaging the scene is linear and therefore superposition holds. The scene is accurately represented by the sum of the individual points of light in the scene. Also, the image is accurately represented by the sum of the blurs resulting from the lens imaging each individual scene point.

Second, it is assumed that the shape of the optical blur (that is, the shape of the *psf*) does not depend on position within the field of view. This is typically not true for optical systems. Typically, optical aberrations vary depending on position in the field of view. The optical blur is generally smaller at the center of an image than at the edge. However, the image plane can generally be subdivided into regions within which the optical blur is approximately constant. A system with constant blur is sometimes called *isoplanatic*.

The assumption here is that the blur caused by the optics (the optical *psf*) is the same anywhere within the region of the image being analyzed. The image of a point source does not change with position. The system is shift-invariant.

Given that the *psf* is constant over the image, then the image can be represented as a convolution of the *psf* over the scene. If $h(x,y)$ represents the spatial shape (the intensity distribution) of the point spread function, then $h(x-x',y-y')$ represents a point spread function at location (x',y') in the image plane. If $s_{cn}(x',y')$ describes the brightness of the object scene and $i_{mg}(x,y)$ is the brightness of the image, then:

$$i_{mg}(x,y) = \int_{-\infty}^{\infty} \int_{-\infty}^{\infty} h(x-x',y-y')s_{cn}(x',y')\,dx'\,dy'. \quad = h(x,y) * s_{cn}(x,y) \quad (2.1)$$

Each point in the scene radiates independently and produces a point spread function in the image plane with corresponding intensity and position. The image is a linear superposition of these point spread functions. Mathematically, that result is obtained by convolving the optical *psf* over the scene intensity distribution to produce the image.

Since a convolution in space corresponds to a multiplication in frequency, the optical system can be considered to be a spatial filter.

$$I_{mg}(\xi,\eta) = H(\xi,\eta)S_{cn}(\xi,\eta) \quad (2.2)$$

where:

$I_{mg}(\xi,\eta)$ = Fourier transform of image

$S_{cn}(\xi,\eta)$ = Fourier transform of scene

$H(\xi,\eta)$ = the Optical Transfer Function (OTF)

ξ and η are spatial frequencies in x and y directions, respectively. The units of ξ and η are cycles per millimeter or cycles per milliradian.

The OTF is the Fourier transform of the point spread function $h(x,y)$. However, in order to keep image intensity proportional to scene intensity, the OTF of the optics is normalized by the total area under the *psf* blur spot.

$$H(\xi,\eta) = \frac{\int\limits_{-\infty}^{\infty}\int\limits_{-\infty}^{\infty} h(x,y)e^{-j2\pi\xi x}e^{-j2\pi\eta y}\,dx\,dy}{\int\limits_{-\infty}^{\infty} h(x,y)\,dx\,dy}. \tag{2.3}$$

The MTF of the optics is the magnitude of the function $H(\xi,\eta)$, $|H(\xi,\eta)|$. The Phase Transfer Function (PTF) can be ignored if the *psf* is symmetrical.

Note that the relationship in Equation 2.2 applies between the scene and the image plane of a well-corrected optical system. The optical system is considered to be "well-corrected" because the *psf*, the optical blur, is reasonably constant over the image plane (i.e., isoplanatic).

Optical systems often have multiple image planes. In this case, the first image becomes the scene which is imaged by the second set of optical elements. For example, the image in Figure 2.1 might be re-imaged by another lens as shown in Figure 2.2. In this case, each point in the original image is blurred by the *psf* of the next set of optics. If the Optical Transfer Function of the second lens is $H_2(\xi,\eta)$, then:

$$I_{mg}(\xi,\eta) = H_2(\xi,\eta)H(\xi,\eta)S_{cn}(\xi,\eta). \tag{2.4}$$

The total system MTF is the product of the individual MTFs.

The transfer function between scene and display is the product of optics MTF, detector MTF, display MTF, and the MTF of other factors which blur the image. Any blurring of the image can be treated as an MTF as long as the blur is constant over the whole image. For example, the active area of a FPA detector acts as optical point spread function. The larger the active detector area, the more blurred the image. In fact, the detector area convolves with the scene to blur the image in the same way that the optical *psf* blurs the image.

It is apparent from Figure 1.2 that the blurring and sampling actions of the detector cannot be physically separated. However, from a mathematical standpoint, the blurring and sampling actions of the detector are considered separately. Sampling is handled in the next chapter. For the present, the detector is viewed as applying a blur to each point in the image.

The MTF of the detector is the Fourier transform of the detector photo-sensitive area. The display MTF is the Fourier transform of a display pixel intensity pattern. In the absence of sampling artifacts, the Fourier transform of the displayed image is the Fourier transform of the scene multiplied by the product of optics, detector, display, and other component MTFs.

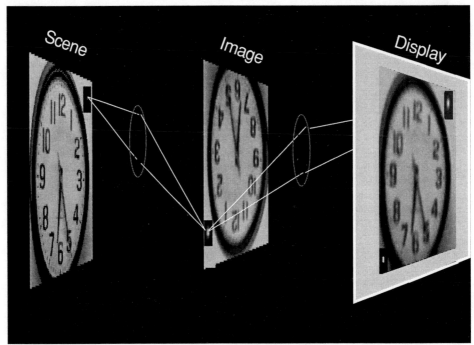

Figure 2.2 Picture is further blurred by imaging with a second lens. The MTF from the scene to the display is the product of the individual lens MTF.

2.2 SPATIAL AND FREQUENCY DOMAIN FILTERS

Equations 2-1 and 2-2 describe the filtering process where one process is in the space domain and the other is in the frequency domain. In space, the output of a linear-shift-invariant (LSI) system is the input convolved with the system impulse response (in this case, the optical *psf*). Take the example given in Figure 2.3. The system shown is a simple imaging system with an input transparency of a four-bar target, an imaging lens, and an output image. Given that the system shown is an LSI system, the output is simply the object convolved with the imaging system impulse response or point spread function. The convolution of the point spread function with the transparency gives a blurred image, as shown.

The spatial domain filtering process shown in Figure 2.3 is equivalent to the frequency domain filtering process shown in Figure 2.4. The two-dimensional Fourier transform of the input function is taken. The input spectrum clearly shows the fundamental harmonic of the four bar target in the horizontal direction. The higher order harmonics are difficult to see in the transform image because the higher order harmonics have much less amplitude than the fundamental.

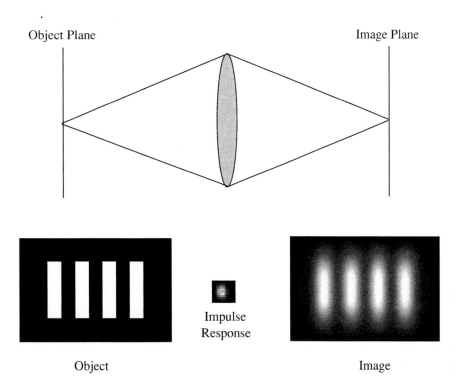

Object Plane   Image Plane

Impulse
Response

Object   Image

Figure 2.3 Spatial filtering in an optical system.

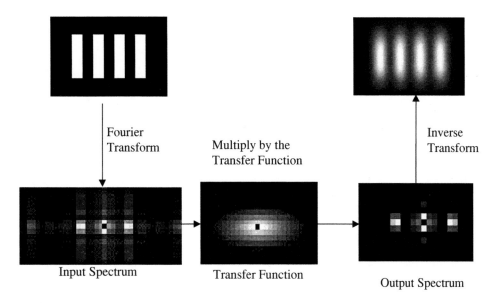

Fourier
Transform

Multiply by the
Transfer Function

Inverse
Transform

Input Spectrum   Transfer Function   Output Spectrum

Figure 2.4 Frequency domain filtering in an optical system.

The transform of the point spread function gives the transfer function of the system. Next, the output spectrum is given by the input spectrum multiplied by the transfer function. Finally, the output image is found by taking the inverse transform of the output spectrum. The resulting image is identical to that given by the spatial convolution of the point spread function in the space domain.

In Figure 2.4, the DC component of the input, transfer, and output frequency spectrums has been removed so that the higher frequency components can be viewed. Otherwise, all that would be seen is a bright point in the middle of the pictures.

To summarize, LSI imaging system analysis can be performed using two methods: spatial-domain analysis and frequency-domain analysis. The results given by these analyses are identical.

2.3 REDUCING LSI IMAGER ANALYSIS TO ONE DIMENSION

It is common in imaging system analysis to analyze sensors in the horizontal and vertical directions. The *psf* and the associated MTF are assumed to be separable in Cartesian coordinates. The separability assumption reduces the analysis one dimension so that complex calculations that include cross-terms are not required. This approach allows straightforward calculations that quickly determine sensor performance.

The separability assumptions are almost never satisfied. Generally, the errors are small, and the majority of scientists and engineers use the separability approximation.

Separability in Cartesian coordinates requires that

$$f(x, y) = f(x)f(y) \tag{2.5}$$

and separability in polar coordinates requires

$$f(r, \theta) = f(r)f(\theta) \tag{2.6}$$

The optical *psf* is a combination of the diffraction spot and the geometric aberrations. Usually, these functions can be characterized by a function that is separable in polar coordinates. The detector *psf* is a rectangular shape that is separable in Cartesian coordinates, but is not separable in polar coordinates. The collective *psf* of the detector and the optics is not separable in either polar or Cartesian coordinates!

Consider an example to illustrate typical errors. Assume an optical aperture of 16.9 cm at a wavelength of 4.0 micrometers to give a diffraction spot that has a radius (from the center of the spot to the first zero) of 0.024 milliradians. The system is diffraction-limited, so that the geometric or aberration blur is negligible. Next, the detector angular subtense (DAS) (the detector width divided by the optics focal length) is 0.034 milliradians in both the horizontal and vertical directions. To determine the collective *psf* of the optics and the detector, the Airy disc and the detector rectangle are convolved. We want to determine the error associated with a one-dimensional approximation of the *psf*.

First, the two-dimensional *psf* is

$$psf(x,y) = (\frac{D}{\lambda})^2 somb(\frac{D\sqrt{x^2+y^2}}{\lambda}) ** \frac{1}{DAS_x DAS_y} rect(\frac{x}{DAS_x}, \frac{y}{DAS_y}) \qquad (2.7)$$

where the ** denotes the two-dimensional convolution. The *somb* function is a circularly symmetric function called the "sombrero" as described by Gaskill since it resembles the hat, but it describes the optical blur. The *somb* function is defined in the later Section 2.4. The *rect* function describes the detector shape and is also defined in Section 2.4. The two-dimensional function described in Equation 2.7 is not separable. Next, calculate the answer for the separable approach where the *psf* is estimated as the combination of two separable functions.

$$psf(x) = \frac{D}{\lambda} somb(\frac{Dx}{\lambda}) * \frac{1}{DAS_x} rect(\frac{x}{DAS_x}) \qquad (2.8)$$

and

$$psf(y) = \frac{D}{\lambda} somb(\frac{Dy}{\lambda}) * \frac{1}{DAS_y} rect(\frac{y}{DAS_y}) \qquad (2.9)$$

Now, the separable *psf* is constructed from the two functions in Equations 2-8 and 2-9.

$$psf(x,y) = [\frac{D}{\lambda} somb(\frac{Dx}{\lambda}) * \frac{1}{DAS_x} rect(\frac{x}{DAS_x})][\frac{D}{\lambda} somb(\frac{Dy}{\lambda}) * \frac{1}{DAS_y} rect(\frac{y}{DAS_y})] \qquad (2.10)$$

The separable and non-separable functions are compared in Figure 2.5. The error can now be determined for the separability assumption (for the optics and detector characteristics stated above). Figure 2.6 shows the difference in the *psf*s. Note that for the parameters given, the maximum difference at any point in space is around 1 percent.

Figure 2.7 shows a comparison between images, one blurred by the non-separable *psf* and the other blurred by the separable *psf*. The top image in the figure is a pristine image that has not been blurred. The image on the lower left has been blurred with the non-separable *psf* given by Equation 2.7. The image on the lower right has been blurred with the separable *psf* given by Equation 2.10. There is no visible difference in the blurring effects on the imagery.

The above example is in the spatial domain, but similar results are obtained in the frequency domain.

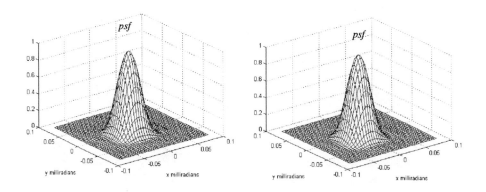

Figure 2.5 Comparison of separable and non-separable *psf*s.

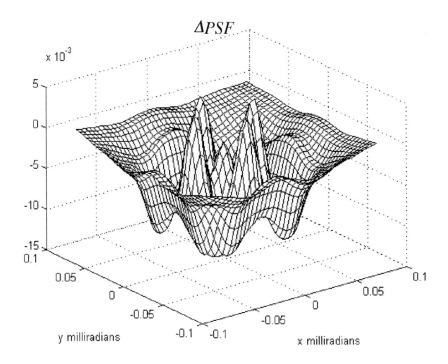

Figure 2.6 Difference in the separable and non-separable *psf*s.

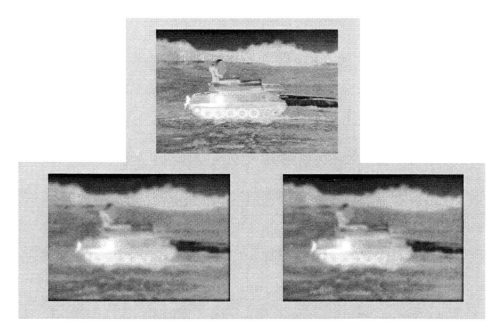

Figure 2.7 Imagery comparing separable and non-separable *psf*s.

In summary, the analysis of imaging systems is usually performed separately in the horizontal and vertical directions. These one-dimensional analyses allow a great simplification in sensor performance modeling. Although the separability assumption is not error-free, the errors usually turn out to be small.

2.4 THE MTF ASSOCIATED WITH TYPICAL IMAGER COMPONENTS

The impulse response or point spread function of an imaging system is comprised of component impulse responses as shown in Figure 2.8. Each of the components in the system contributes to the blurring of the scene. The blur attributed to a component may be comprised of more than one physical effect. For example, the optical blur is a combination of the diffraction and aberration effects of the optical system. The point spread function of the system is a convolution of the individual impulse responses:

$$h_{system}(x,y) = h_{atm}(x,y) **h_{optics}(x,y) **h_{det}(x,y) **h_{elec}(x,y) **h_{disp}(x,y) **h_{eye}(x,y)$$

(2.11)

The Fourier transform of the system impulse response is called the *transfer function* of the system. Since a convolution in the spatial domain is a product in the frequency domain:

$$O(\xi,\eta) = I(\xi,\eta)H_{atm}(\xi,\eta)H_{optics}(\xi,\eta)H_{det}(\xi,\eta)H_{elec}(\xi,\eta)H_{disp}(\xi,\eta)H_{eye}(\xi,\eta).$$ (2.12)

The system transfer function is the product of the component transfer functions.

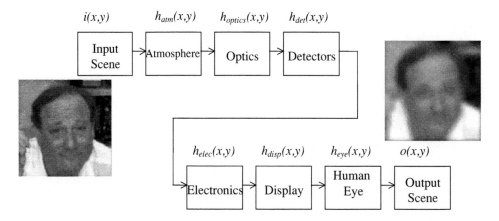

Figure 2.8 System *psf* results from convolving the individual *psf* of all of the system components.

Detailed descriptions of the point spread functions and modulation transfer functions for typical imager components are given below.

2.4.1 Optical filtering

There are two filters that account for the optical effects in an imaging system: diffraction and aberrations. The diffraction filter accounts for the spreading of the light as it passes an obstruction or an aperture. The diffraction impulse response for an incoherent imaging system with a circular aperture of diameter D is

$$h_{diff}(x,y) = (\frac{D}{\lambda})^2 somb^2(\frac{Dr}{\lambda}) \tag{2.13}$$

where λ is the average band wavelength and r is the square root of x^2 plus y^2. The *somb* (for sombrero) function is:

$$somb(r) = \frac{J_1(\pi r)}{\pi r} \tag{2.14}$$

where J_1 is the first order Bessel function of the first kind. The filtering associated with the optical aberrations is sometimes called the geometric blur. There are many ways to model this blur and there are numerous commercial programs for calculating geometric blur at different locations on the image. However, a convenient method is to consider the geometric blur collectively as a Gaussian function

$$h_{geom}(x,y) = \frac{1}{r_{geom}^2} Gaus(\frac{r}{r_{geom}}), \tag{2.15}$$

where r_{geom} is the geometric blur scaling factor. The Gaussian function, *Gaus*, is

$$Gaus(r) = e^{-\pi r^2} \tag{2.16}$$

Note that the scaling values in front of the *somb* and the *Gaus* functions are intended to provide a functional volume (under the curve) of unity so that no gain is applied to the scene. Examples of the optical impulse responses are given in Figure 2.9 corresponding to a wavelength of 10 micrometers, an optical diameter of 10 centimeters, and a geometric blur of 0.1 milliradians.

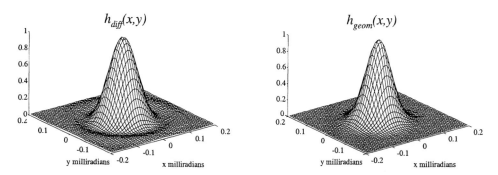

Figure 2.9 Spatial representations of optical blur. Diffraction blur is shown on the left and geometric blur on the right.

The overall impulse response of the optics is the combined (convolved) blur of both the diffraction and aberration effects

$$h_{optics}(x, y) = h_{diff}(x, y) ** h_{geom}(x, y). \tag{2.17}$$

The transfer functions corresponding to the above impulse responses are obtained by taking the Fourier transform of the functions given in Equations 2.13 and 2.15. The Fourier transform of the *somb* is:

$$H_{diff}(\xi, \eta) = \frac{2}{\pi}[\cos^{-1}(\frac{\rho\lambda}{D}) - (\frac{\rho\lambda}{D})\sqrt{1 - (\frac{\rho\lambda}{D})^2}] \tag{2.18}$$

where

$$\rho = \sqrt{\xi^2 + \eta^2}$$

and is in units of cycles per milliradian. The Fourier transform of the *Gaus* function is simply the *Gaus* function, with care taken on the scaling property of the transform. The transfer function corresponding to the aberration effects is

$$H_{geom}(\xi, \eta) = Gaus(r_{geom}\rho). \tag{2.19}$$

The somb and Gaus transfer functions are shown in Figure 2.10. The overall optical transfer function is the product of the two functions.

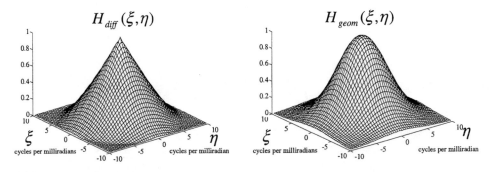

Figure 2.10 Optical transfer functions. The MTF of the diffraction blur is shown on the left, and the MTF of the geometric blur is shown on the right.

2.4.2 Detector spatial filters

Two spatial filtering effects are normally associated with the detector. The first is associated with spatial integration over the detector active area. Spatial integration over the detector area occurs for both scanning and staring sensors. The second occurs in sensors where the detector is scanned across the scene. In this case, the relative motion between scene and detector results in a motion blur. The extent of the blur depends on how far the detector moves while the signal is being integrated by the electronic circuitry. Typically, the detector signal is integrated for a period of time, the integrated signal is sampled, and then the integrator is reset. The integrate and hold circuit is generally called a "sample and hold" circuit.

$$h_{\det}(x,y) = h_{\det\_sp}(x,y) ** h_{\det\_sh}(x,y) \tag{2.20}$$

Other effects can be included, but are usually negligible. For example, variation in detector responsivity will affect the spatial MTF of the detector, but responsivity is generally uniform over the active area of the detector.

The detector spatial impulse response is due to the spatial integration of the light over the detector. Since most detectors are rectangular, the rectangle function is used as the spatial model of the detector

$$h_{\det\_sp}(x,y) = \frac{1}{DAS_x DAS_y} rect(\frac{x}{DAS_x}, \frac{y}{DAS_y})$$
$$= \frac{1}{DAS_x} rect(\frac{x}{DAS_x}) \frac{1}{DAS_y} rect(\frac{y}{DAS_y}) \tag{2.21}$$

where DAS_x and DAS_y are the horizontal and vertical detector angular subtenses in milliradians. The detector angular subtense is the detector width (or height) divided by the sensor focal length.

PSF=h ~ detector width   width h↑, H↓
F[h] = H   width of
                            fct for large detector
                            width h↑, H↓

Fourier integral representation of an optical image   **35**

The MTF corresponding to the detector spatial integration is found by taking the Fourier transform of Equation 2.21.

$$H_{det\_sp} = \text{sinc}(DAS_x \xi)\ \text{sinc}(DAS_y \eta) \tag{2.22}$$

e.g. $DAS_x = 0.1\ mrad$

where the sinc function is defined as

$$\text{sinc}(\pi x) = \frac{\sin(\pi x)}{(\pi x)}. \tag{2.23}$$

$\frac{1}{0.1} = 10\ cyc/mrad$

The impulse response and the transfer function for a detector with a 0.1 by 0.1 milliradian detector angular subtense is shown in Figure 2.11.

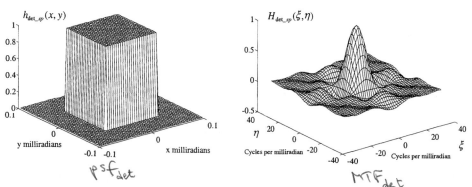

psf_det   MTF_det

Figure 2.11 Detector spatial impulse response and transfer function.

In parallel scan thermal imagers, the scene is mechanically scanned across a linear array of detectors. Each detector generates a line of video as the field of view of the sensor is scanned. In older sensors, the analog detector outputs were amplified and then processed in various ways to construct the displayed image. In most modern parallel scan imagers, circuitry on the detector focal plane integrates the photoelectron signal for a sample time period. At the end of the sample period, the integrator voltage is read out by a sample and hold circuit. The integrator is then reset in preparation for the next sample.

The detector sample and hold function is an integration of the detector photoelectron signal as the scene is scanned across the detector array. Because the scene is moving relative to the detector during the integration period, the sample and hold circuit represents a spatial integration (or spatial blur) of the image. This image blurring is in addition to the spatial integration of the detector itself. It is important to note that this additional blurring does not occur for staring sensors, because the scene is not scanned across the staring array during the integration of the photo-signal.

The scan direction is assumed to be the horizontal or *x* direction. Usually, the distance in milliradians between samples is smaller than the detector angular subtense (the instantaneous field of view) by a factor called *samples per DAS* or *samples per IFOV*, ϑ. The sample and hold function is a rectangular function in x where the size of the rectangle corresponds to the distance between samples. In the vertical or y direction, the function is an impulse function. Therefore, the impulse response of the sample and hold circuit is:

$$h_{det\_sh}(x,y) = \frac{\vartheta}{DAS_x} rect(\frac{x\vartheta}{DAS_x})\delta(y). \qquad (2.24)$$

The Fourier transform of the impulse response gives the transfer function of the sample and hold operation

$$H_{det\_sh}(\xi,\eta) = sinc(\frac{DAS_x\xi}{\vartheta}). \qquad (2.25)$$

The Fourier transform of the impulse function in the y direction is 1. The impulse response and the transfer function for a sample and hold (two samples per detector DAS) associated with the detector in Figure 2.11 are shown in Figure 2.12.

$\vartheta = 2$

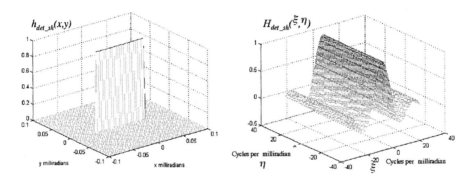

Figure 2.12 Detector sample and hold impulse response (left) and transfer function (right).

2.4.3 Electronic filtering

The electronic filtering function is one of the more difficult to characterize and one of the more loosely applied functions. First, it involves the conversion of spatial frequencies to temporal frequencies. Second, most impulse response functions are even. That is, they are symmetrical about the origin and the resulting MTF is real. With electronic filtering, the impulse function is one-sided because the *psf* cannot go backwards in time. The resulting MTF is complex; it has imaginary as well as real parts. Nonetheless, to avoid dealing with complex numbers, the electronic filtering is normally represented with a real MTF. This violates causality, but the resulting errors tend to be small. This approximation does not usually have a heavy impact on sensor performance estimates since the electronics are not typically the limiting component of the sensor. The analyst should be careful to understand, however, that the electronics cannot be accurately modeled in this manner. Section 2.5 addresses temporal filtering in more detail.

2.4.4 Display filtering

The finite size and shape of the display spot also corresponds to a spatial filtering of the image. Usually, the display pixel (the blur spot) for a cathode ray tube (CRT) has a Gaussian intensity distribution whereas the pixel for a flat panel display is rectangular in shape. Light emitting diode displays also have rectangularly shaped pixels. The *psf* of the display is simply the size and shape of the display spot. The finite size, shape and intensity distribution of the display spot must be converted from a physical dimension on the display surface to sensor angular space.

For the Gaussian spot, the spot size dimension in centimeters must be converted to an equivalent angular space in the sensor's field-of-view

$$\sigma_{angle} = \sigma_{cm} \frac{FOV_v}{L_{disp}} \qquad (2.26)$$

where L_{disp} is the length in centimeters of the display vertical dimension and FOV_v is field-of-view of the sensor in milliradians (see Figure 2.13). For the rectangular display element, the height and width of the display element are converted to the sensor's angular space in the same way.

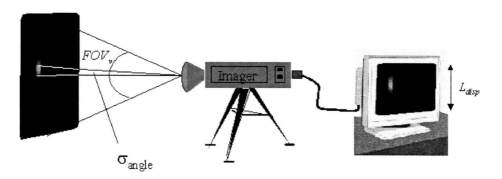

Figure 2.13 Conversion of CRT spot size to angular coordinates.

Once these angular dimensions are obtained, the *psf* of the display spot is simply the size and shape of the display element:

$$h_{disp}(x,y) = \frac{1}{\sigma_{angle}^2} Gaus(\frac{r}{\sigma_{angle}}) \qquad \text{for a Gaussian spot} \qquad (2.27)$$

or

$$h_{disp}(x,y) = \frac{1}{W_{angle}H_{angle}} rect(\frac{x}{W_{angle}}, \frac{y}{H_{angle}}) \quad \text{for flat panel} \qquad (2.28)$$

where the angular display element shapes are given in milliradians.

The transfer functions associated with these display spots are determined by taking the Fourier transform of the above *psf* equations.

$$H_{disp}(\xi,\eta) = Gaus(\sigma_{angle}\rho) \quad \text{for Gaussian display} \qquad (2.29)$$

and

$$H_{disp}(\xi,\eta) = sinc(W_{angle}\xi, H_{angle}\eta) \quad \text{for flat panel display.} \qquad (2.30)$$

2.4.5 Filtering by the human eye

The human eye has a *psf* that is a combination of three physical components: optics, retina, and tremor (see Overington). In terms of these components, the *psf* is

$$h(x,y) = h_{eye\_optics}(x,y) ** h_{retina}(x,y) ** h_{tremor}(x,y) \qquad (2.31)$$

The transfer function of the eye is important in calculating human performance when using a sensor system.

The transfer function of the eye is:

$$H_{eye}(\xi,\eta) = H_{eye\_optics}(\xi,\eta) H_{retina}(\xi,\eta) H_{tremor}(\xi,\eta) \qquad (2.32)$$

The transfer function of the eye optics is a function of display light level. This is because the pupil diameter changes with light level. The number of foot-Lamberts, fL, at the eye from the display is Ld/0.929 where Ld is the display luminance in milli-Lamberts. The pupil diameter is then

$$D_{pupil} = -9.011 + 13.23\exp\{-\log_{10}(fL)/21.082\} \text{ [millimeters].} \qquad (2.33)$$

This equation is valid if one eye is used as in some targeting applications. If both eyes view the display, the pupil diameter is reduced by 0.5 millimeters. There are two parameters, *io* and *fo*, that are required for the eye optics transfer function. The first parameter is

$$io = (0.7155 + 0.277/\sqrt{D_{pupil}})^2 \qquad (2.34)$$

and the second is

$$fo = \exp\{3.663 - 0.0216 D_{pupil}^2 \log(D_{pupil})\} \qquad (2.35)$$

Now, the eye optics transfer function can be written

$$H_{eye\_optics}(\rho) = \exp\{-(43.69(\rho/M)/fo)^{io}\} \qquad (2.36)$$

where ρ is the radial spatial frequency,

$\sqrt{\xi^2 + \eta^2}$, in cycles per milliradian

and M is the imaging system magnification. In Figure 2.13, the magnification would be the angular subtense the display subtends to an observer divided by the imager FOV. Note that M depends on display height and observer viewing distance.

The retina transfer function is:

$$H_{retina}(\rho) = \exp\{-0.375(\rho/M)^{1.21}\} \qquad (2.37)$$

Finally, the transfer function of the eye due to tremor is:

$$H_{tremor}(\rho) = \exp\{-0.4441(\rho/M)^2\} \qquad (2.38)$$

which completes the eye model.

As an example, let the magnification of the system equal 1. With a pupil diameter of 3.6 millimeters corresponding to a display brightness of 10 fL and viewing with one eye, the MTF of the eye is shown in Figure 2.14. The *io* and *fo* parameters were 0.742 and 27.2, respectively.

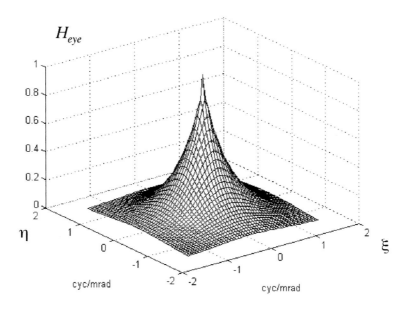

Figure 2.14 Eye transfer function.

2.5 TEMPORAL FILTERS

Consider the imaging system shown in Figure 2.15. A target (a single bar) is imaged by a lens onto an image plane. A detector scans across the image plane and the output of the detector is an electrical signal that represents the intensity variation across the image on the line scanned by the detector. The variation in the electrical signal is related to the spatial variation by the scan velocity. A spatial frequency in cycles per milliradian is converted to Hertz by multiplying by the scan velocity

$$f = \xi v \quad \text{Hertz (Hz)} \tag{2.39}$$

where v is the scan velocity in milliradians per second and ξ is spatial frequency in cycles per milliradian. The circuit is usually an amplifier and a filter. The circuit drives a display monitor.

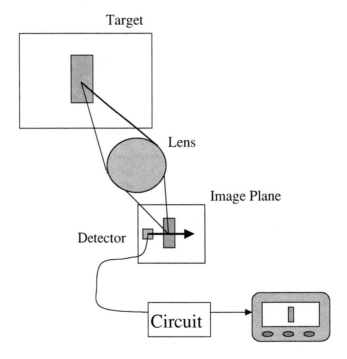

Figure 2.15 Diagram of scanning sensor showing electronic circuit between the detector and display.

The diffraction of the lens, the detector shape, the sample-and-hold, the monitor display spot, and the eye all blur the original target. The circuit also blurs the target. Like the other imager components, the circuit has an impulse response and a transfer function. However, the impulse response of the circuit is different from the impulse response of the optics or detector or display.

Electronic circuits are different from other imager components because they are *causal*: the output cannot be affected by an input which has yet to occur. The impulse response for a circuit must be one-sided. When a lens blurs a point source of light, the blur generally spreads in all directions from the point source. A electronic circuit can only blur forward in time.

In order to explore the impulse response of the circuit, consider an image plane with no diffraction blur, no detector shape blur (i.e., an infinitesimal detector size), and a perfect display. Therefore, the blur introduced by the circuit is the only blur seen on the display.

In this example, the electronics is a low pass filter. Consider the circuit shown in Figure 2.16 and the square wave input voltage shown in the figure. The input voltage is a scan of the bar target (with infinitesimal detector size) converted to time by the scan velocity. The target is a rectangular bar which produces a quick rise in detector voltage and then a quick drop in detector voltage. The detector voltage is the circuit input signal, and the circuit output voltage is driving the display.

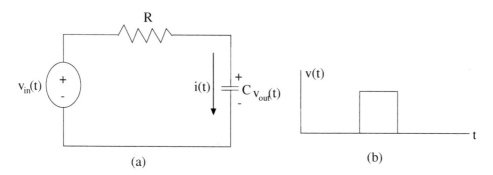

Figure 2.16 Low pass filter (a) and input signal (b).

In the analysis of the low pass circuit, Kirchoff's voltage equation gives

$$-v_{in}(t) + \frac{1}{C}\int_0^t i(t) + i(t)R = 0 \tag{2.40}$$

where the initial current is zero. Taking the Fourier transform of the equation gives

$$V_{in}(\omega) = \frac{1}{jwC} I(\omega) + I(\omega)R. \tag{2.41}$$

The current spectrum in the circuit can be determined from Equation 2.42.

$$I(\omega) = \frac{V_{in}(\omega)}{R + 1/j\omega C}. \tag{2.42}$$

The output voltage spectrum is simply the current spectrum times the impedence of the capacitor

$$V_{out}(\omega) = \frac{V_{in}(\omega)}{R + 1/j\omega C} 1/j\omega C .$$

(2.43)

The transfer function of the circuit is the ratio of the output spectrum over the input spectrum.

$$H(\omega) = \frac{V_{out}(\omega)}{V_{in}(\omega)} = \frac{1}{1 + j\omega RC}.$$

(2.44)

The impulse response is determined by taking the inverse Fourier transform of the transfer function

$$h(t) = \frac{1}{RC} e^{-t/RC} step(t).$$

(2.45)

The impulse response of a low pass filter is an exponential decay starting at the time the circuit is stimulated. Part of every input is delayed forward in time, nothing is propagated backward in time.

Equation 2.45 is the function that is convolved with the detector output to give the response of the electronics. In Figure 2.17, a perfect image of a rectangular bar is shown on the left. The output which results from convolving the bar image with the impulse response is shown on the right. An intensity trace for one scan line is shown at the top of the figure.

The amount of electronics blur in Figure 2.17 is exaggerated. The electronics of an imaging system usually imparts only a small amount of blur on the image compared to the effects of detector shape and optical blur. The impact of electronic filtering is purposely exaggerated in order to be easily visible.

The one-sided nature of electronic blur has several implications. First, the image is offset, delayed, by the electronics. In this example, the image is shifted to the right. If a bi-directional scan mirror is used, then the image is alternately offset to the left and then right, and this leads to an image breakup that must be corrected by other circuitry or by the display.

Another characteristic unique to circuits is that the Fourier transform of the impulse response must be complex (have both real and imaginary parts). Only symmetrical impulse functions can be represented by a real MTF. Although complex transfer functions are certainly handled by the theory, complex math makes calculations more difficult. Since, in a well-designed imager, the electronics has little actual effect on the image, real MTFs are generally assumed. It is generally assumed that the electronics will mildly degrade high frequency imager response and that any phase artifacts can be ignored.

Assuming a real MTF, however, implies that the impulse response of the circuit is two-sided and that no delay (no shifting) of the image has occurred. There are many artifacts in real scanning imagers that cannot be analyzed correctly by using a real MTF to represent the electronic transfer function. If, for any reason, the electronics is an important factor affecting image quality, then the electronics must be analyzed with the correct, complex, transfer function.

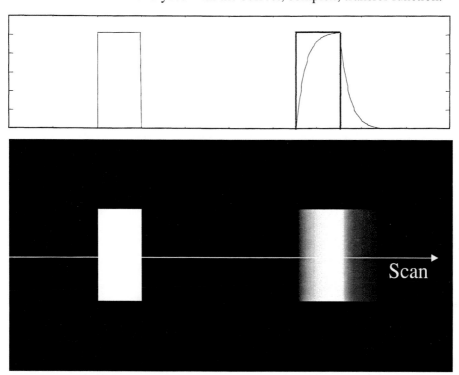

Figure 2.17 The impulse response of an electronic circuit is causal: an output cannot precede the input which causes it. At bottom, the bar on the left is scanned by a detector from left to right and the detector signal is passed through a low pass circuit and then displayed on the right. The intensity variation of a scan line through the center of the bar is shown at the top of the figure. Since the detector is scanning left-to-right, all blur occurs to the right of the bar.

BIBLIOGRAPHY

Boreman,, G. B., *Basic Electro-Optics for Electrical Engineers*, SPIE Tutorial Text, Bellingham, WA, 1998.

Driggers, R., P. Cox, and T. Edwards, *Introduction to Infrared and Electro-Optical Systems*, Artech House, Norwood, MA, 1999.

Gaskill, J., *Linear Systems, Fourier Transforms, and Optics,* Wiley, New York, NY, 1978.

O'Neill, E., *Introduction to Statistical Optics*, Addison-Wesley, Reading, MA, 1963.

Overington, I., *Vision and Acquisition,* Crane, Russak, New York, NY, 1976.

Pinson, L., *Electro-Optics,* Wiley, New York, NY, 1985.

3

SAMPLED IMAGER RESPONSE FUNCTION

In this chapter, the response function for a sampled imager is derived. The sampled imager response function quantifies the transfer response of the sampled system; that is, it describes how well the desirable scene content is preserved within the image. The response function also quantifies the sampling artifacts which will be visible in the image.

The procedure for finding the sampled imager response function exactly parallels the procedure described in Chapter 2 for finding the transfer response for a non-sampled imager. The sampled imager response function is the Fourier transform of the imager point spread function. As discussed in Chapter 1, the point spread function of a sampled imager is not shift-invariant; it varies depending on position within the field of view of the sensor. The sampled imager response function is more complicated than the transfer function for a non-sampled system. This is because it contains information about both the transfer response of the system plus information about the sampling artifacts.

The sampled imager response function depends on the sensor pre-sample MTF, the sample spacing, and the post-sample or display MTF. These sensor characteristics are known to the design engineer or system's analyst. The sampled imager response function does not depend on the image samples, but rather on the process by which the samples are taken and displayed.

Since the sampling artifacts produced by an imager depend on the scene being imaged, one might question a mathematical process which quantifies sampling artifacts without including an explicit description of the scene. In that regard, we rely on assumptions identical to those used for non-sampled imagers.

As discussed in Chapter 2, MTF is used to characterize a non-sampled imager. MTF is the Fourier transform of the displayed point spread function. It describes the blur produced in the image by a point in the scene. In actual usage, the importance of a good MTF response at high frequency cannot be established until the high frequency content of the scene is established. The real impact or importance of the sensor blur is not known until the scene content is known. Nonetheless, MTF has proven to be a good indicator of the overall utility of the sensor. The ability of a non-sampled imager to resolve high frequency content in the scene is generally important when using the imager. High frequency response in a non-sampled imager is a prized characteristic because of the possibilities it provides, not because good MTF is always important in accomplishing every task when looking at any scene.

Experience has shown that MTF is a good way to characterize the quality of an imaging system. An image cannot be defined until the scene is described, but the characterization of the imager's response to a point source provides a good indication of the quality of images which can be expected under a variety of environments.

A similar logic applies to sampled imagers. We cannot know how each detail in the scene will be corrupted by the sampling process until the scene itself is specified. However, the *tendency* of the imager to produce visible display raster or corrupt scene details can be characterized.

In this chapter, Fourier theory is used to describe sampled imaging systems. A response function for sampled imagers is derived by examining the image formed on the display by a point source of light in the scene. The response function provides a quantitative way to characterize both the quality of the sampled imager's transfer response and its tendency to generate sampling artifacts.

3.1 FOURIER TRANSFORM OF A SAMPLED IMAGE

The image plane in Figure 2.1 is now sampled. As discussed in the last chapter, it is assumed that the point spread function and its Fourier transform are separable in Cartesian coordinates (x,y). The image is sampled in the x-direction while holding y constant; y is then incremented and another row of samples taken. In this manner, the whole, two-dimensional image is sampled. Separability is assumed, so the two-dimensional transform is the product of the separate Fourier transforms in the x and y directions. The small errors associated with the separability assumption are also discussed in Chapter 2.

Figure 3.1 shows the clock before blurring by the lens. Figure 3.2 shows an intensity trace taken along the white line drawn in Figure 3.1. Figure 3.3 shows the clock blurred by the lens, and Figure 3.4 shows the resulting intensity trace. It is the blurred intensity pattern in Figure 3.4 which is sampled. In a real sensor, the image would be blurred by the detectors and perhaps by other factors such as line of sight jitter or motion blur. The actual pre-blur and sampling process is discussed in Chapter 1; see Figures 1.2 and 1.3 in particular. In this conceptual example, the optical blur is a stand-in for all of the possible pre-sample blurs.

Figure 3.5 shows the pre-sampled image $f(x)$ sampled in the x-direction with spacing X. The image is sampled throughout space. Only a finite number of samples are non-zero because the image itself is finite. The answer from sampling all space will equal the answer from sampling a finite interval only if $f(x)$ is zero outside the sampled interval. In the following, the Fourier transform of the pre-sampled image is the transform of the *sampled part* of the image. This distinction is only important if $f(x)$ is thought to represent a whole scene, only

Figure 3.1 Clock picture before it is blurred by the lens in Figure 2.1. The plot in Figure 3.2 below shows intensity along the white line.

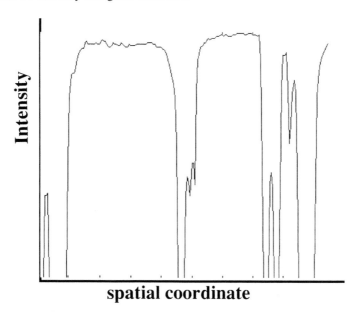

Figure 3.2 Plot of the intensity along the white line shown in Figure 3.1. Notice the high frequency content indicated by sharply rising and falling lines and significant intensity variation over a small spatial interval.

Figure 3.3 Clock imaged and blurred by the lens shown in Figure 2.1.

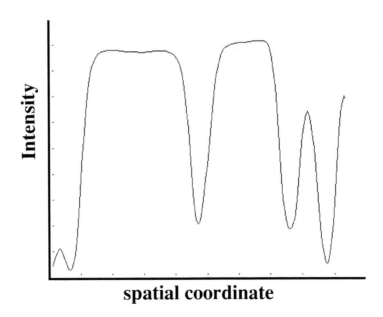

Figure 3.4 Intensity plot of the blurred image taken along the white line shown in Figure 3.3. Notice that intensity varies less in each spatial interval; the intensity rise and fall is less sharp.

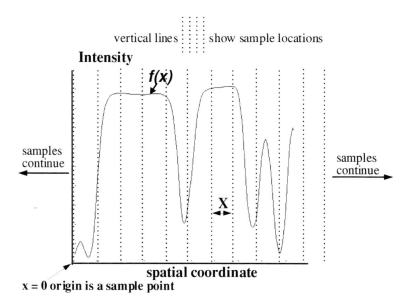

vertical lines show sample locations

Figure 3.5 Blurred image *f(x)* is sampled at points indicated by dashed, vertical lines. Sample spacing is *X* and sampling continues throughout all space. The *x* = 0 origin is a sample point.

part of which is sampled. In the derivation below, *f(x)* must represent only the sampled part of the scene, and $F(\xi)$ is the Fourier transform of that limited (windowed) *f(x)*.

The *x* = 0 origin is a sample point. The origin of the scene is offset by a distance *d*; this allows the sample phase to be explicitly included in the mathematical derivation. That is, we want the mathematics to tell us what happens when the pre-sample image is moved with respect to the sample points. The pre-sample signal, *f(x)*, could be defined as whatever the intensity pattern is in the coordinate system of the samples. This would appear to simplify the derivation. However, in such a case, *f(x)* must be re-defined every time the sensor moves or rotates relative to the scene. The constant re-definition of *f(x)* would obscure the relationship between the scene, the sample phase, and the final displayed image.

The pre-sampled image *f(x)* is formed by convolving the point spread function of the lens *h(x)* with the scene $s_{cn}(x)$.

$$f(x) = \int_{-\infty}^{\infty} h(x - x')s_{cn}(x' - d)dx'$$

$$f(x) = h(x) * s_{cn}(x - d)$$

(3.1)

where * indicates convolution.

The mathematical derivation below parallels the derivation presented in Section 1.5.3 of Chapter 1. The image is sampled by multiplying the pre-sampled

CCD

image by a comb of delta (impulse) functions. The displayed image is then reconstructed by convolving the display pixel shape with the delta function samples. Let $p_{ix}(x)$ be the intensity distribution associated with a single display pixel and $P_{ix}(\xi)$ be its Fourier transform. The displayed image is represented by

$$i_{dsp}(x) = \{[h(x)*s_{cn}(x-d)]\cdot\sum_{n=-\infty}^{\infty}\delta(x-nX)\}*p_{ix}(x). \tag{3.2}$$

Because a convolution in the space domain is a multiplication in the frequency domain and vice-versa, we can write:

$$I_{dsp}(\xi) = \Big[(H(\xi)S_{cn}(\xi)e^{-j2\pi\xi d} * \sum_{n=-\infty}^{\infty}\delta(\xi-n\nu)]P_{ix}(\xi)\Big] \tag{3.3}$$

where ν is the sample frequency $(1/X)$ with units of cycles per millimeters or cycles per milliradian.

$$I_{dsp}(\xi) = P_{ix}(\xi)\sum_{n=-\infty}^{\infty}H(\xi-n\nu)S_{cn}(\xi-n\nu)e^{-j2\pi(\xi-n\nu)d}$$

$$I_{dsp}(\xi) = P_{ix}(\xi)\sum_{n=-\infty}^{\infty}F(\xi-n\nu)e^{-j2\pi(\xi-n\nu)d} \tag{3.4}$$

where $F(\xi)$ equals $H(\xi)\,S_{cn}(\xi)$ because $f(x)$ is defined by Equation 3.1 to be the convolution of $h(x)$ with $s_{cn}(x)$. That is, the Fourier transform of the pre-sampled image is the MTF of the sensor times the Fourier transform of the scene. The displayed frequency spectrum is illustrated in Figure 3.6. The sampling process replicates the pre-sample image spectrum $F(\xi)$ at each integer multiple of the sample frequency. The displayed spectrum is the product of the replicated spectra multiplied by the display pixel MTF.

The Fourier transform of the sampling artifacts is the product of the display MTF times all of the replicated spectra except the one located at the frequency origin (the one for $n = 0$). Figure 3.6 only shows the amplitude of the spectra; phase is not shown. Each replicated spectrum, however, varies in phase from the adjacent spectrum by the sample phase increment $2\pi d/X$ because:

$$\Delta\phi = \text{change in phase between replicas}$$
$$\Delta\phi = 2\pi(\xi-(n-1)\nu)d - 2\pi(\xi-n\nu)d$$
$$\Delta\phi = 2\pi\nu d \tag{3.5}$$
$$\Delta\phi = 2\pi d/X.$$

As sample phase varies, the displayed spectrum will vary.

In Equation 3.4, the sampled signal contains the same transfer response as a non-sampled imager. That is, the $n = 0$ term is $P_{ix}(\xi)H(\xi)S_{cn}(\xi)$, which represents the product of the sensor and display MTFs multiplied by the Fourier transform of the scene. This term represents the desired frequency content in the image. This desirable frequency content is often refered to as the *baseband spectrum* or simply *baseband*.

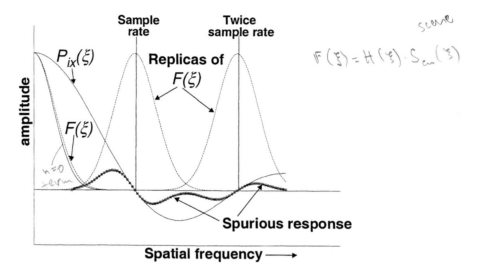

Figure 3.6 The pre-sample image spectrum $F(\xi)$ is replicated at all integer multiples of the sample frequency. The displayed image spectrum is the product of the display MTF $P_{ix}(\xi)$ and all of the replicated spectra including the original $F(\xi)$ at the spatial frequency origin. The Fourier transform of the sampling artifacts is that part of the image spectrum that is found by multiplying the display MTF by all of the replicated spectra except the one located at the origin. This product is called the spurious response of the sampled imager.

In this tutorial, the entire part of the image spectrum which results from sampling, other than the baseband spectrum itself, is called *spurious response*. The spurious response is the sum of all the terms in Equation 3.4 except the $n = 0$ term. The spurious response is the Fourier transform of the sampling artifacts in the image.

The term spurious response is a synonym for <u>*aliasing*</u>. Aliasing correctly refers to the entire part of the displayed image spectrum that results from the replicated or "aliased" spectra. We have defined another term for the aliased response because using the word aliasing to represent the entire spurious spectrum which results from sampling would be confusing to many readers.

It has become common practice among engineers to use the term "aliasing" to refer only to overlap in the frequency domain between the sample generated replica spectra and the baseband spectrum. Ideally, aliasing which does not overlap the baseband spectrum [does not overlap $F(\xi)$] can be removed by post-sample filtering. However, even near-ideal filters are difficult to implement, and removing such artifacts as visible raster from an image often entails degrading the baseband response. In most sampled imagers, aliased frequency content can and does exist at frequencies above the effective zero cutoff of $F(\xi)$.

In order to avoid confusion, the entire part of the image spectrum which results from sampling, other than the baseband spectrum, will be referred to as *spurious response*. In frequency space, the spurious response is the Fourier transform of the sampling artifacts.

3.2 DERIVATION OF THE SAMPLED IMAGER RESPONSE FUNCTION

The response function $R_{sp}(\xi)$ for a sampled imager is found by examining the impulse response of the system. The response function is the Fourier transform of the image formed on the display by a point source in the scene. The procedure is identical to that used with non-sampled systems, but the result will be different because sampled systems are not shift-invariant.

The function being sampled is $h(x)$, the point spread function of the pre-sampled image. Therefore, based on Equation 3.4:

$$R_{sp}(\xi) = P_{ix}(\xi) \sum_{n=-\infty}^{\infty} H(\xi - n\nu) e^{-j2\pi(\xi - n\nu)d}. \qquad (3.6)$$

The replicas of $H(\xi)$ which are centered at two or more times the sample frequency are normally filtered out by the display and eyeball MTF because of their high frequency content. In most practical systems, only the replicas adjacent to the baseband (with $n = \pm 1$) contribute visible sampling artifacts. This typical situation is represented in Figure 3.7. Also, the phase factor which is common between terms, the $e^{-j2\pi\xi d}$ factor, is dropped, since it provides no insight into system amplitude response. Equation 3.6 can be simplified by writing out the sum and dropping the terms with $n > 1$:

$$R_{sp}(\xi) \approx P_{ix}(\xi) \sum_{n=-1}^{1} H(\xi - n\nu) e^{j2\pi n\nu d}$$

$$R_{sp}(\xi) \approx P_{ix}(\xi) H(\xi) + P_{ix}(\xi) H(\xi - \nu) e^{j2\pi\nu d} + P_{ix}(\xi) H(\xi + \nu) e^{-j2\pi\nu d} \qquad (3.7)$$

$$R_{sp}(\xi) \approx P_{ix}(\xi) H(\xi) + P_{ix}(\xi) H(\xi - \nu) e^{j\phi} + P_{ix}(\xi) H(\xi + \nu) e^{-j\phi}$$

where ϕ, the sample phase, $= 2\pi d / X$. In some unusual cases, the terms with $n = \pm 2$ or higher can contribute to the spurious response, and Equation 3.7 needs to be modified to include those terms.

The response function has two parts, the transfer term and the spurious response terms. The first term in Equation 3.7 is the transfer response of the imager. This transfer response does not depend on sample spacing, and it is the only term that remains for small sample spacing. A sampled imager has the same transfer function as a non-sampled (that is, a very well-sampled) imager.

However, a sampled imager always has the additional response terms, which we refer to as *spurious response*. These spurious response terms in Equation 3.7

are filtered by the display MTF, $P_{ix}(\xi)$, in the same way that the transfer response is filtered. However, the position of the spurious response terms on the frequency axis depends on the sample spacing. If the sample spacing is large (the sample frequency is small), then the spurious response terms lie close to the baseband in frequency space. In this case, the spurious response is difficult to filter out and might even overlap the baseband. If the sample spacing is small (the sample frequency is high), then the spurious response terms lie far from the baseband in frequency space and the spurious response is filtered out by the display and eyeball MTF.

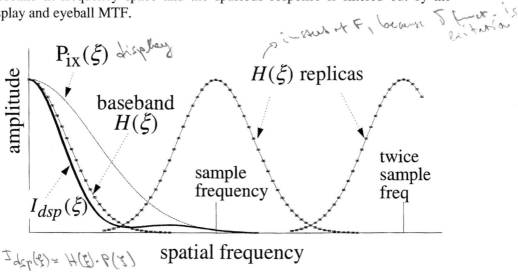

$$I_{dsp}(\xi) = H(\xi) \cdot P(\xi)$$

Figure 3.7 Typically, the display and eye MTF cannot filter out the sampling replicas adjacent to the baseband but do an effective job of filtering out the higher order replica spectras.

Figures 3.6 and 3.7 only show the amplitudes of the transfer and spurious responses, but the sample phase in Equation 3.7 must not be ignored. The phase relationship between the transfer response and the spurious response depends on the sample phase. This means that the displayed image changes depending on the exact relationship between the sensor and the scene. A small angular movement of the sensor changes the sample phase, and that results in a different display frequency (phase) spectrum. Remember that a sampled imager is not shift-invariant. That means that, as the sensor is panned across the scene, the displayed image changes depending on sample phase. That change in display frequency spectrum (that change in the intensity pattern on the display) is due to the changing sample phase in Equation 3.7.

Eye MTF can be an important factor in limiting the visibility of both the transfer response and spurious response. When analyzing a sensor and display system, $P_{ix}(\xi)$ should generally include the eye MTF. It should be remembered that the effect of eye MTF depends on system magnification. The frequency used when calculating eye MTF is the object space frequency divided by system magnification.

Factors such as figure size, reader viewing distance, and figure print quality cannot be predicted or controlled by the author of a book. In many of the examples that follow, the display pixels are large in order to minimize the impact of the unknown viewing conditions. With large display pixels, the eye MTF can be ignored. Therefore, the eye MTF is not included in some of the response function calculations that are presented below.

3.3 EXAMPLES OF SAMPLED IMAGER RESPONSE FUNCTIONS

Following are some examples which illustrate the kind of information that can be gleaned from the sampled imager response function. In these examples, the amplitudes of the transfer and spurious response terms are plotted, and the relationship between the response function plots and image characteristics is discussed.

It should be remembered that the transfer and spurious terms in Equation 3.7 are complex, and the amplitude of the entire function at any one frequency is not the sum of the amplitudes of the individual terms. If the replicas of the pre-sample MTF overlap, then determining the amplitude of $R_{sp}(\xi)$ at any one frequency in the overlap region requires a complex summation of all the terms, and the result will depend on sample phase.

When the amplitudes of the transfer and spurious terms are plotted, only the positive (right-hand) frequency plane is sometimes shown. Since the image is real, the transfer and spurious terms must be symmetrical about the frequency origin. In many cases, the $P_{ix}(\xi)H(\xi+\upsilon)e^{-i\phi}$ term (the spurious term on the negative frequency axis) will be negligible for $\xi > 0$ and the spurious response will plot as a single term on the positive frequency axis. However, this is not always the case. Sometimes the spurious term, or even multiple terms, from the negative frequency axis spreads over to the positive axis and vice-versa.

In the following examples, $P_{ix}(\xi)$ is real; that is, the display pixel shape is symmetrical. A real MTF can take on negative values. Multiplying a complex function by a negative real value changes the phase of the function by 180 degrees. In the following figures, plotting a portion of a transfer or spurious term as negative indicates a 180 degree phase shift.

Chapter 4 will provide metrics to quantify the effect of sampling on visual task performance. As will be discussed in Chapter 4, the degree to which sampling affects task performance depends on the nature of the visual task as well as on the nature of the sampling artifacts. The examples in this chapter are meant to illustrate the connection between the spurious response terms and the presence and nature of visible sampling artifacts. The examples in this chapter do not relate to quantifying the loss in performance due to those visible artifacts.

3.3.1 Example 1: The pictures of Lena in Chapter 1

The original picture of Lena shown in Figure 1.5(a) was blurred to produce Figure 1.5(b). The blur was generated by convolving with both a Gaussian and a rect function. The Gaussian fell to 10% amplitude at a half width of four pixels. The rect function was eight samples wide. The image was down-sampled 8:1 both horizontally and vertically. The reconstruction in Figure 1.5(d) was done with square display pixels.

Figure 3.8 shows the transfer and spurious response terms for the picture of Lena in Figure 1.5(d); the display MTF used to make Figure 1.5(d) is also shown in Figure 3.8. The large, square display pixels lead to considerable out-of-band spurious response in the image. The high frequency content permitted by these display pixels makes it difficult for the eye and visual system to integrate the underlying image.

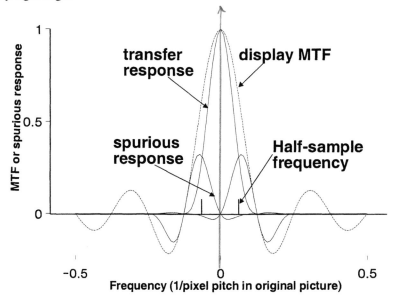

Figure 3.8 Transfer and spurious response and display MTF for the Lena picture shown in Figure 1.5(d). The large, square display pixel leads to considerable spurious response beyond the half-sample rate. The frequency content beyond half the sample rate represents the blocky, distinct display pixel edges seen in the picture in 1.5(d).

The picture in Figure 1.7 was constructed using the display MTF shown in Figure 3.9; the transfer and spurious response terms associated with Figure 1.7 are also shown in that figure. The display MTF now removes the high frequency content. The picture in Figure 1.7 is better than the picture in Figure 1.5(d). Figure 1.7 does not look as good as Figure 1.5(b) because the spurious response overlaps the transfer response, corrupting the image. Also, the display MTF adds additional blur to the image, lowering the transfer response.

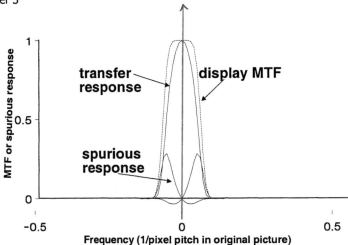

Figure 3.9 Transfer and spurious response and display MTF for the Lena picture shown in Figure 1.7. The display MTF filters out most frequency content beyond the half-sample rate. Most of the degradation between Figure 1.7 and Figure 1.5(b) is due to the spurious response which overlaps the transfer response and corrupts the image (baseband aliasing). Also, the display MTF used to generate Figure 1.7 adds blur to the image.

The improvement between Figures 1.5(d) and 1.7 results from using more addressable display pixels in 1.7 than in 1.5d. The picture in Figure 1.5(d) could result from large, square display pixels or could result (as it did) from using pixel replication to zoom the image. The "display MTF" in Figure 3.9 actually resulted from a combination of digital image processing plus actual display pixel characteristics. This topic is discussed in detail in the next chapter.

Figures 3.8 and 3.9 show both the negative and positive sides of the frequency axis. Notice the symmetry. It is often convenient to show only the positive side. Notice also, however, that the spurious term on the negative axis can actually extend into the positive half plane and vice-versa.

3.3.2 Example 2: Effect of changing sample rate

This example starts with the picture of the clock shown in Figure 3.1; the picture was taken with a charge-coupled-device (CCD) television camera. The horizontal and vertical MTF were measured and are shown in Figure 3.10. The sampling rate of the CCD camera is 1.67 cycles per milliradian (cy/mrad) both horizontally and vertically.

This example illustrates the impact of changing sample rate while holding other sensor and display parameters constant. In this example, the pre-sample and post-sample MTF are held constant and only the sample rate is varied.

The pre-sample MTF caused by the camera does not change just because fewer samples are used to reconstruct the image. Holding the pre-sample MTF

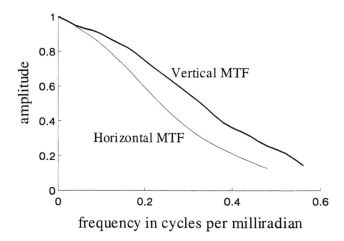

Figure 3.10   Measured horizontal and vertical MTF for camera used in clock example.

constant is easy. In order to hold the post-sample MTF constant, while varying the sample spacing, the display pixel shape cannot change. Since the display pixels must be large enough to fill in the image at the lowest sample rate, the pixels must overlap at the higher sample rates. This is illustrated in Figure 3.11.

In Figure 3.11(a), each square pixel is aligned side-by-side. At the lowest sample rate, the pixel size (width and height) equals the pixel pitch. In Figure 3.11(b), the large display pixels are still used to reconstruct the image; this keeps the post-sample MTF constant. However, in the cases where the samples are closer together, the display pixels overlap. This overlap of adjacent pixels when the sample spacing is less than the pixel dimension is illustrated in Figure 3.11(b). Overlap between adjacent display pixels blurs the image; the blur increases as the overlap increases.

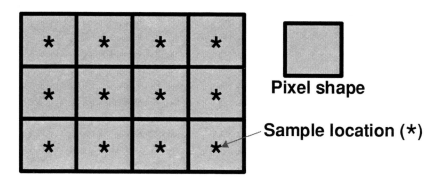

Figure 3.11(a)   The clock images were reconstructed with square pixels. The pixel size is such that, at the lowest sample rate, the pixels just touch at each edge.

Even pixels

Odd pixels

Figure 3.11(b) In the following clock examples, the higher sample rate images are reconstructed with display pixels that overlap. The overlap is illustrated above in one dimension, but in the examples the pixels overlap in both the horizontal and vertical direction. Each sample is reconstructed with a large, square display pixel, and when the samples are close together, the large display pixels overlap, blurring the image. Keeping the pixel size constant keeps the MTF constant between the examples where the sample rate is varied.

The display pixels are large enough that they are contiguous at the lowest sample rate. At the higher sample rates, the display pixels overlap. This keeps the display pixel size and shape the same between examples which use different sample spacings. A single display pixel is shown in the upper right corner of each picture.

The display pixel has been made large in order to minimize the impact of viewing condition. The display pixel shown at the upper right of each picture should appear large and square to the viewer. Eye MTF has not been factored into the display MTF in this example.

Figure 3.12 shows the clock image down-sampled by two in each direction. That is, every other sample from the original image shown in Figure 3.1 is discarded both horizontally and vertically. One quarter as many samples are used to generate Figure 3.12 as are used to generate Figure 3.1. The sample rate is now 0.83 cy/mrad in both directions. In Figure 3.12, unlike Figure 3.1, large, square display pixels are used. The image in Figure 3.12 is blurry. The display pixels overlap because they are large compared to the sample spacing. The sample spacing is one-quarter of a display pixel dimension in each direction.

Figure 3.13 shows the camera MTF and the replicated spectrum centered at the new sample rate of 0.83 cy/mrad. Replicated spectra at other multiples of the sample frequency are present but not shown. The display MTF is also shown in Figure 3.13. The display pixel is essentially square with a size in object space of 4.8 milliradians; therefore, the display MTF is a sinc wave that cuts off (first MTF zero) at about 0.2 cycles per milliradian.

The horizontal and vertical transfer and spurious responses associated with Figure 3.12 are shown in Figure 3.14. The picture in Figure 3.12 is blurry because the MTF of the large display pixel creates a significant drop in the

Figure 3.12   Clock image sampled at 0.83 cy/mrad and displayed using large, square pixels as shown in the upper, right-hand corner. The large display pixels overlap, blurring the image.

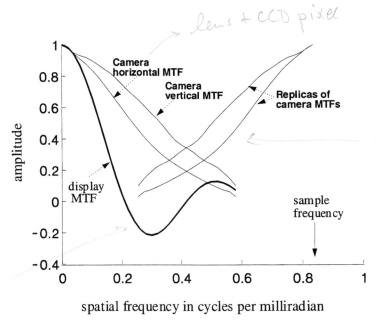

Figure 3.13   Graph shows replicas of camera MTF located at multiples of 0.83 cycles per milliradian (the sample rate in Figure 3.12). The display MTF is also shown.

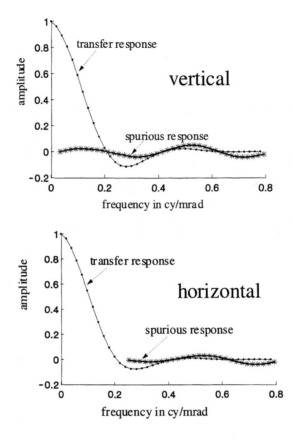

Figure 3.14   Transfer and spurious response for the camera under the sampling and display conditions associated with Figure 3.12. The picture is blurry because the large display pixel limits the transfer response to 0.2 cy/mrad. Note, however, that the spurious response is mostly filtered out by the display; significant sampling artifacts are not present. This is because the first pre-sample MTF replica is located at 0.83 cy/mrad; this is a high enough frequency that the display MTF filters it out.

transfer response. The transfer response is dominated by the 0.2 cy/mrad cutoff of the display. However, sampling artifacts are not apparent. As seen in Figure 3.14, spurious response is almost zero everywhere on the frequency axis. The MTF replica which causes the spurious response is centered at the sample frequency of 0.83 cycles per milliradian and is therefore well filtered by the MTF of the large display pixel.

In Figure 3.15, the clock picture in Figure 3.1 is now down-sampled by four in each direction. The sample spacing is now one-half of a pixel dimension in each direction. The display pixels still overlap, but not as much as in the previous example shown in Figure 3.12. The shape and size of the display pixel has not changed, but the sample spacing has been increased by a factor of two in each direction. The image is clearly interpretable, but sampling artifacts have appeared. Some edges are jagged, pixel intensities on the numbers are incorrect, and some of the minute markings are missing or out of place.

Figure 3.16 shows the camera horizontal MTF, the pre-sample MTF replicas due to sampling at the new sample rate, and the display MTF. In order to reduce clutter in the figure, the vertical MTF and its replicas are not shown. The sample rate is now 0.42 cy/mrad and replicas of the pre-sample MTF are spaced closer together than in Figure 3.13 because they are spaced at multiples of this smaller sample frequency. Part of the pre-sample MTF replica centered on the negative side of the frequency origin, the $P_{ix}(\xi)H(\omega+\upsilon)e^{-i\phi}$ term in Equation 3.7, now spreads to the positive side of the frequency axis. The part of the $P_{ix}(\xi)H(\omega+\upsilon)$ $e^{-i\phi}$ term visible on the positive side of the frequency axis is labeled $e^{-i\phi}$.

Figure 3.17 shows the horizontal and vertical transfer and spurious responses for the sample spacing used in Figure 3.15. The transfer response is the same as in the previous example, but the spurious response has changed; it is worse. Since spurious response is now at lower frequencies due to the lower sample rate, it is not filtered out as effectively by the display MTF. Also, notice that the spurious response shown in Figure 3.17 is in two parts, because the $P_{ix}(\xi)H(\omega+\upsilon)e^{-i\phi}$ term (from the negative side of the frequency axis) contributes. As noted above, the $P_{ix}(\xi)H(\xi+\upsilon)e^{-i\phi}$ term spreads over to the positive frequency axis (and vice-versa) when the sample spacing gets small. As a short-hand notation in the figure, the spurious term from the MTF replica centered at the sample frequency on the positive half of the frequency axis is labeled as $e^{+i\phi}$, and the spurious term from the MTF replica centered at the sample frequency on the negative half of the frequency axis is labeled $e^{-i\phi}$.

In Figure 3.15, the minor changes in detail (variations in intensity, line widths, etc.) are due to the overlap between the spurious response and the transfer response. This overlap between spurious and transfer responses is shown in Figure 3.17. Further, due to the sinc wave nature of the display MTF, the spurious response beyond the half-sample rate is not removed. The spurious response at high frequencies, beyond the half-sample frequency, contributes the jagged edges and blockiness seen in the image.

Figure 3.18 shows the clock image down-sampled eight times in both directions; the sample spacing is now equal to the size of the display pixel in each dimension. Again, the transfer response has not changed; this is because the camera MTF and display pixel MTF are the same as in the two previous clock examples. Because of the lower sample rate, the blockiness and jagged edges are more apparent than in the previous example. Also, the corruption of the baseband is much worse; parts of the image are completely missing or substantially changed. These picture characteristics can be explained by looking at Figures 3.19 and 3.20.

Figure 3.19 shows that the replicated spectra is now centered at multiples of 0.21 cy/mrad, the new sample frequency. The horizontal and vertical transfer and spurious responses are shown in Figure 3.20. The low frequency spurious

Figure 3.15 Clock image in Figure 3.1 down-sampled by four in each direction; sample frequency is now 0.42 cy/mrad. The display pixel has not changed from Figure 3.12. Sampling artifacts have appeared. The intensity and thickness of lines varies across the picture, and some of the minute markings are missing completely.

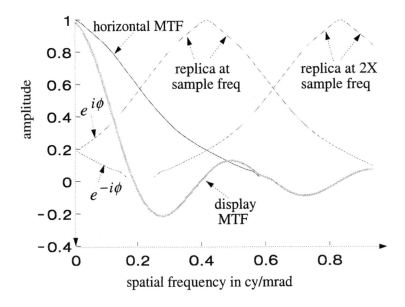

Figure 3.16 This figure shows horizontal camera MTF and replicas resulting from sampling at 0.42 cy/mrad. Since the first replica is now centered at a lower frequency, it is not filtered as effectively by the display MTF. Also, the MTF replica on the negative side of the frequency axis [the $P_{ix}(\xi)H(\xi+\upsilon)e^{-i\phi}$ term in Equation 3.7] becomes visible as it spreads to the positive side of the frequency axis. In the figure, the MTF replica on the positive half of the frequency axis is labeled as $e^{+i\phi}$, and the portion of the replica from the negative half of the frequency axis is labeled $e^{-i\phi}$.

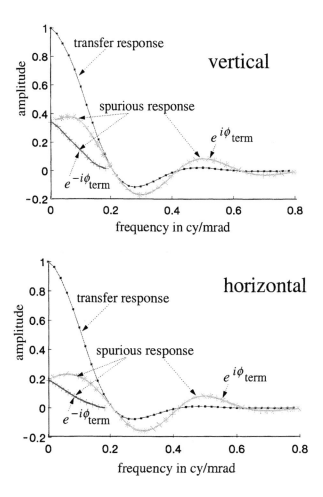

Figure 3.17 Transfer and spurious response for the camera under the sampling and display conditions associated with Figure 3.15. Notice that the spurious response is in two parts, because the $P_{ix}(\xi)H(\xi+\upsilon)e^{-i\phi}$ term from the negative side of the frequency axis contributes. In the figure, the spurious term from the positive half of the frequency axis is labeled as $e^{+i\phi}$, and the spurious term from the negative half of the frequency axis is labeled $e^{-i\phi}$. The baseband content is somewhat corrupted due to the overlap of spurious and transfer response. The blocky nature of the image is due to the higher frequency, spurious content.

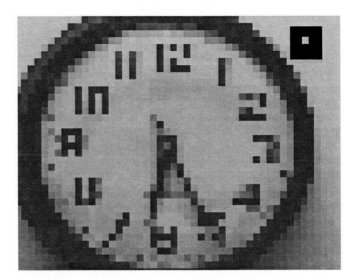

Figure 3.18 Clock image in Figure 3.1 down-sampled by eight in each direction. Sample frequency is now 0.21 cy/mrad. The sample pitch now equals the pixel size, whereas in Figures 3.12 and 3.15, adjacent pixels overlapped. Because of the lower sample rate, parts of the image are missing or substantially changed due to aliasing. Also, the blocky nature of the display pixels is now visible.

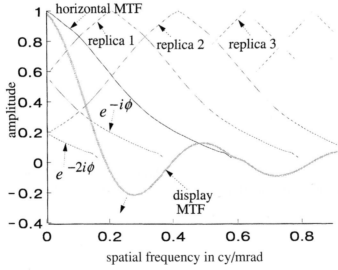

Figure 3.19 This figure shows horizontal camera MTF and replicas resulting from sampling at 0.21 cy/mrad. The display MTF cannot filter out the spurious response because the MTF replicas which lead to spurious response are now at low frequencies. The MTF replica at twice the sample rate on the negative half of the frequency axis is labeled as $e^{-2i\phi}$, and the replica at the sample frequency on the negative half of the frequency axis is labeled $e^{-i\phi}$.

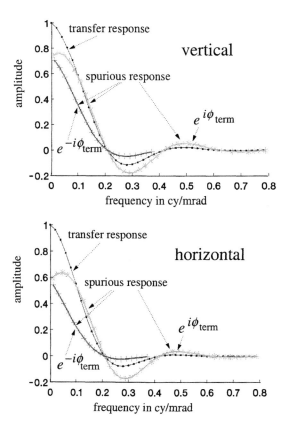

Figure 3.20 Transfer and spurious response for the camera under the sampling and display conditions associated with Figure 3.18. Note that the spurious response, which is generated by the MTF replica which is centered at the sample rate of 0.21 cy/mrad, seriously overlaps the transfer response and therefore corrupts the image content. The blockiness (the sharply defined pixels edges) in the image is indicated by the higher frequency, spurious content.

response is about as large as the transfer response, causing significant corruption of the basic image information. Also, the high frequency spurious response is quite large, meaning that the sharp pixel edges are quite visible.

Comparing Figures 3.12, 3.15, and 3.18, the images do not look more blurry as the sample rate decreases. On the contrary, although the pictures become increasingly more corrupted, the images appear sharper as sample rate decreases due to the increased high frequency content of the spurious response.

3.3.3 Example 3: Midwave infrared sensor

The last example illustrates the application of the sampled imager response function to a midwave infrared sensor design. In this case, the pre-sample blur includes optical diffraction and detector shape. The sensor is a 3 to 5 micrometer imager with a 5 centimeter focal length, and the diameter of the objective lens is

2.2 centimeters. The detector size is 31 micrometers square and the distance between detector centers is 38 micrometers. With a 256 by 256 detector staring array, the field of view of the system is 11 by 11 degrees.

The sampled spectrum shown in Figure 3.21 is calculated using this information and the transfer functions given in Chapter 2. The detector angular subtense is 0.62 milliradians and the sample rate is 1.32 samples per milliradian ✓ (the half-sample rate is 0.66 cycles per milliradian). Only the horizontal spectrum is shown since the vertical spectrum is identical.

The post-sample or reconstruction blur is generated by the display monitor spot size and the eye blur. The display spot width is 0.035 centimeters (standard deviation of the Gaussian shape) and the display height is 15.24 centimeters. The distance of the display to the eye is 30 centimeters giving a magnification of 2.61. The post-sample MTF, labeled "Total" in Figure 3.22, is shown along with the display and the eye MTF.

The post-sample MTF is multiplied by the sampled spectrum of Figure 3.21 in order to determine the transfer response and the spurious response. These functions are shown in Figure 3.23. The transfer response results from multiplying the post-sample MTF by the pre-sample MTF. The pre-sample MTF is the sample-replicated spectrum which is centered at the frequency origin in Figure 3.21. The spurious response results from multiplying the post-sample MTF by the sample-replicated spectra not centered at the frequency origin.

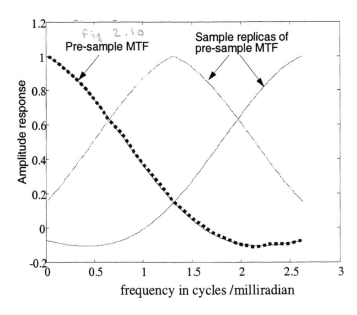

Figure 3.21 This figure shows the pre-sample MTF and the sampled spectrum for the example midwave sensor.

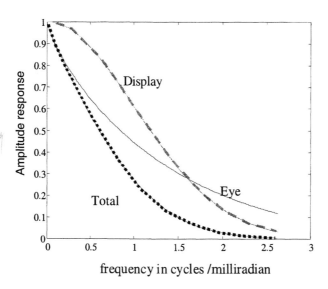

Figure 3.22 The "Total" MTF shown in the figure is the post-sample or reconstruction MTF for this example. The post-sample or reconstruction MTF results from multiplying the display MTF by the eye MTF.

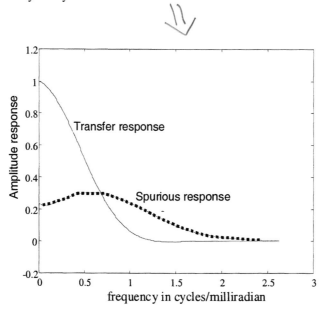

Figure 3.23 The sensor transfer (baseband) response results from multiplying the total post-sample MTF shown in Figure 3.22 by the pre-sample MTF (the single component of the replicated spectrum which is centered at the frequency origin) in Figure 3.21. The sensor spurious response results from multiplying the total post-sample MTF shown in Figure 3.22 by those components of the replicated spectrum not centered at the frequency origin (labeled "sample replicas of pre-sample MTF" in Figure 3.21).

Such a sensor and display system might benefit from a smaller display MTF (bigger display spot) to control the high frequency spurious response. However, this control of sampling artifacts would be at the expense of the transfer response. Removing the spurious response that lies just above the half-sample frequency by increasing display blur would also blur the image content below the half-sample frequency. An even better enhancement would be to interpolate with an electronic post process in order to control the spurious response beyond the half-sample frequency with little degradation to the transfer response. This technique is described in the next chapter.

3.4 DEFINITION AND CALCULATION OF THE SPURIOUS RESPONSE RATIO

The transfer and spurious response functions of a sampled imager can be calculated using Equation 3.7. These response functions provide the Fourier transform of the baseband (desirable) spatial image information and the Fourier transform of the sampling artifacts, respectively. The sampled imager response function mathematically describes the imaging behavior of the system. However, in predicting the effect of sampling on task performance, the response function must somehow be condensed into a sampling-goodness metric for the sensor. Some generalizations must be made and a goodness factor or factors calculated.

Three aggregate quantities are defined which have proven useful in predicting how the spurious response of a sampled imaging system affects task performance. The utility of these quantities was discovered during experiments looking at the effect of sampling on target acquisition performance. The experiments and the utility of these quantities are described in the next chapter. The quantities are defined here because of their close relationship to the sampled imager response function described by Equation 3.7. The three quantities are: total integrated spurious response ratio, SR, as defined by Equation 3.8, in-band spurious response ratio, $SR_{in-band}$, as defined by Equation 3.9, and out-of-band spurious response ratio, $SR_{out-of-band}$ as defined by Equation 3.10.

$$SR = \frac{\int_{-\infty}^{\infty} |P_{ix}(\xi)|[H^2(\xi-v)+H^2(\xi+v)]^{1/2} d\xi}{\int_{-\infty}^{\infty} |P_{ix}(\xi)H(\xi)| d\xi} \tag{3.8}$$

$$SR_{in-band} = \frac{\int_{-v/2}^{v/2} |P_{ix}(\xi)|[H^2(\xi-v)+H^2(\xi+v)]^{1/2} d\xi}{\int_{-\infty}^{\infty} |P_{ix}(\xi)H(\xi)| d\xi} \tag{3.9}$$

$$SR_{out\text{-}of\text{-}band} = SR - SR_{in\text{-}band}.$$ (3.10)

The spurious response ratio, SR, is the integral over all frequencies of the spurious response normalized by the integral of the transfer response. It is the integrated bad signal divided by the integrated good signal. In-band spurious response ratio ($SR_{in\text{-}band}$) is the integral of all the spurious response at frequencies less than the half-sample frequency normalized by the integral of the transfer response. The out-of–band spurious response ratio ($SR_{out\text{-}of\text{-}band}$) is the integral of spurious response at frequencies greater than the half-sample frequency normalized by the integral of the transfer response. Later in this tutorial, the quantities SR, $SR_{in\text{-}band}$ and $SR_{out\text{-}of\text{-}band}$ are used to quantify the impact of sampling when using a sampled imager for target acquisition.

In the following example of a spurious response calculation, both the pre-sample blur and post-sample or reconstruction blur are Gaussian. The Gaussian pre-sample blur is scaled such that the half-width to the $\exp(-\pi)$ point occurs at 1.3 milliradians and the $\exp(-\pi)$ point for the reconstruction blur is 1.1 milliradians. The sample spacing of the pre-blur is set at 1 milliradian. The sampled spectrum and the post-sample or display MTF (the dashed line) of this system is shown in Figure 3.24.

The transfer response is derived by multiplying the pre-sample MTF by the display MTF. The spurious response is derived by multiplying all the replicas of the pre-sample MTF (except for the original which is centered at the frequency origin) by the display MTF. The transfer and spurious response functions are shown in Figure 3.25.

The total spurious response ratio, defined by Equation 3.8, is found by integrating the area under the spurious response curve and then dividing that area by the area under the transfer response curve. This is illustrated in Figure 3.25, where the area under the spurious response curve is cross-hatched. The cross-hatched area is divided by the area under the transfer response curve to arrive at the total spurious response ratio. In this example, the total spurious response ratio, SR, is 0.217.

The in-band spurious response ratio, $SR_{in\text{-}band}$, is calculated by integrating the area of the spurious response function for frequencies less than the half-sample rate normalized to the transfer response area. This is illustrated in Figure 3.26. The out-of-band spurious response ratio, $SR_{out\text{-}of\text{-}band}$, is $SR - SR_{in\text{-}band}$. In this example, the half-sample rate is 0.5 cycles per milliradian, and the in-band spurious response ratio is calculated to be 0.087. The out-of-band spurious response is calculated to be 0.130.

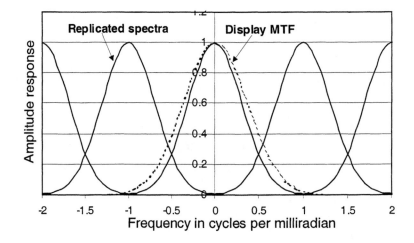

Figure 3.24 Sampled spectrum and display MTF for spurious response ratio example. Both the pre-blur and post-blur are Gaussian. The dotted line shows the post-sample (display) MTF. Sample frequency is 1.0 cycles per milliradian, so the half-sample rate is 0.5 cycles per milliradian.

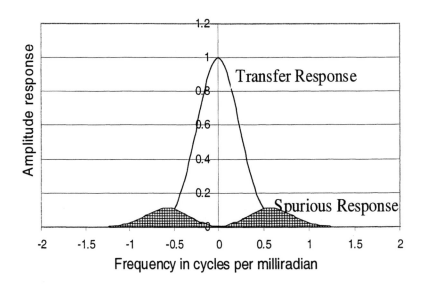

Figure 3.25 Transfer and spurious responses resulting from the sampled spectrum and display MTF shown in Figure 3.24. The total spurious response ratio is found by integrating the area under the spurious response curve (the hatched area in this figure), and then dividing by the area under the transfer response curve.

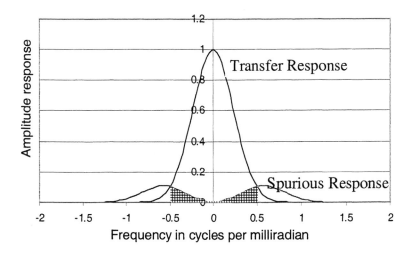

Figure 3.26 The in-band spurious response ratio is found by integrating the area under the spurious response curve for frequencies between minus half and plus half the sample rate (the hatched area in this figure) and then dividing by the area under the transfer response curve. The out-of-band spurious is the total spurious response minus the in-band response ratio.

BIBLIOGRAPHY

Driggers, R., R. Vollmerhausen, B. O'Kane, "Character Recognition as a Function of Spurious Response," *Journal of the Optical Society of America A*, Vol. 16, No. 5, May, 1999.

Legault, R., "The Aliasing Problems in Two-Dimensional Sampled Imagery," in *Perception of Displayed Information* (L.Biberman, Ed.), Plenum Press, New York, NY, 1973.

Oppenheim, A. V. and R. W. Schafer, *Digital Signal Processing,* Prentice-Hall: Englewood Cliffs, NJ, 1975.

Park, S. K. and A. Schowengerdt, "Image Sampling, Reconstruction, and the Effect of Sample-Scene Phasing," *Applied Optics*, Vol. 21, No. 17, p. 3142.

Petersen, D. and D. Middleton, "Sampling and Reconstruction of Wave-Number-limited Functions in N-Dimensional Euclidean Spaces," *Information and Control*, Vol. 5, p. 279-323, 1962.

Schade, O., "Image Reproduction by a Line Raster Process," in *Perception of Displayed Information* (L.Biberman, Ed.), Plenum Press, New York, NY, 1973.

Vollmerhausen, R., "Impact of Display Modulation Transfer Function on the Quality of Sampled Imagery," *SPIE* Aerospace/Defense Sensing and Controls, Vol. 2743, p. 12-22, 1996.

Vollmerhausen, R., R. Driggers, and B. O'Kane, "The Influence of Sampling on Target Recognition and Identification," *Optical Engineering*, Vol. 38, No. 5, May, 1999.

Wittenstein, W., J.C. Fontanella, A.R. Newberry, and J. Baars, "The Definition and the OTF and the Measurement of Aliasing for Sampled Imaging Systems," *Optica Acta*, Vol. 29, No. 1, p. 50.

Wozencraft, J. M. and I.M. Jacobs, *Principles of Communication Engineering*, Wiley, New York, NY, 1965.

4

SAMPLED IMAGER DESIGN AND OPTIMIZATION

The way an image is processed and displayed is just as important as the blur and sampling characteristics of the sensor. In this chapter, the importance of interpolation and image reconstruction is demonstrated. The classical design rules for sampled imaging systems are reviewed. A new method for optimizing the design of sampled systems, the "MTF Squeeze" approach, is presented. Finally, three exercises are provided where MTF Squeeze is used to optimize the design of imaging systems.

4.1 INTERPOLATION AND IMAGE RECONSTRUCTION

The sampling artifacts associated with out-of-band spurious response can be removed by the display or image reconstruction process. Multiple display pixels per sensor sample are used, and the sensor samples are interpolated to provide the intensity values for the added pixels. It is possible to remove essentially all of the out-of-band spurious response with little degradation to the transfer response of the sensor. That is, image interpolation can remove much of the bad without affecting the good; there does not need to be a degradation caused by the interpolation process.

Interpolation requires some amount of image processing, and the display must have more than one pixel per sensor sample. So, there may be a system cost or complexity penalty for interpolation.

Interpolation enhances the fidelity of the displayed image. From a spatial-domain viewpoint, the reconstructed image should match the pre-sampled image between samples. Large, rectangular or square display pixels have sharply defined edges; these visible edges represent spurious content which did not exist in the pre-sample image. On the other hand, large, Gaussian shaped display pixels tend to average the image between samples, blurring and softening the image. However, a mathematical interpolation can provide a good estimate of the pre-sample intensity pattern between the sensor samples. Multiple, smaller display pixels can then be used to generate the correct intensity pattern on the display.

From a frequency-domain viewpoint, the display and any associated signal processing should provide a filter that discriminates against the spurious response while retaining the baseband transfer response. Large, distinct, rectangular or square pixels generate spurious, high frequency content. Large pixels with a more blurred, Gaussian shape degrade the transfer response of the system. If the display can have multiple pixels per sensor sample, then signal processing techniques can be used to reduce the spurious response without degrading the transfer response.

If the display provides one pixel per sensor sample, then the post filter characteristics, $P_{ix}(\xi)$ in Equation 3.7, are set by the design of the display. The display pixel shape and spacing, in combination with the eye MTF, determine the relative amount of transfer and spurious response in the final image. The pixel shape and spacing might be such as to provide a pleasing image, but generally the result will be sub-optimal. For example, if the display pixels are large (that is, visible to the eye) and rectangular, then the image will be degraded by the resulting spurious response, similar to that previously shown in Figure 1.5(d).

A display with large, rectangular pixels is not uncommon. Low resolution, flat panel displays have this characteristic. It is also common practice to enlarge or "zoom" an image by replicating pixels. That is, the picture is doubled in size horizontally by making each new pixel equal to its neighbor to the left, and then the picture is doubled in size vertically by making each new pixel equal to the neighbor above. If the system is eye limited because the display is small, then the larger picture provided by pixel replication will allow the observer to see more of the details in the original sensor image. However, in many cases, replication is repeated until the display pixels are easily seen by the eye; these large, rectangular display pixels have poor display properties. The spurious content generated by the visible pixel edges hides the underlying image.

The benefits of image reconstruction using multiple, non-replicated, display pixels for each sensor sample will be illustrated with an example. The original image at top left of Figure 4.1 is blurred by optics and detector and is shown at top right in Figure 4.1. The sampled and reconstructed image is shown at the bottom left. The image under consideration has a Gaussian pre-sample blur of 10 milliradians half-width, a sample spacing of 10 milliradians, and a rectangular display element that fills the distance between samples.

The sampled spectrum and the display MTF are shown in Figure 4.2. The baseband response and the spurious response are shown in Figure 4.3. The rectangular shaped display element has a sinc transfer function, where the first zero occurs at the sample rate. This broad-band display MTF results in a large amount of out-of-band spurious response. The in-band spurious response is 0.23 and the out-of-band spurious response is 0.75.

With such a large out-of-band spurious response, it makes sense to perform an interpolation. This operation involves doubling the display element count and interpolating values between existing samples. The new rectangular display element is half the dimension of the previous element, thus making the display

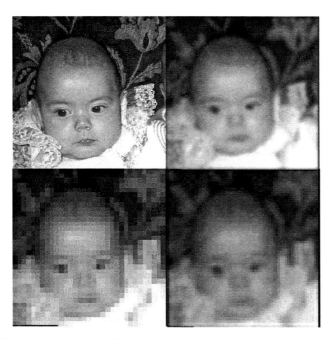

Figure 4.1 Original scene at top left is blurred and shown at top right. After sampling, rectangular display pixels are used for reconstruction at bottom left. Picture at bottom right uses twice as many rectangular pixels (each half the size of those at bottom left).

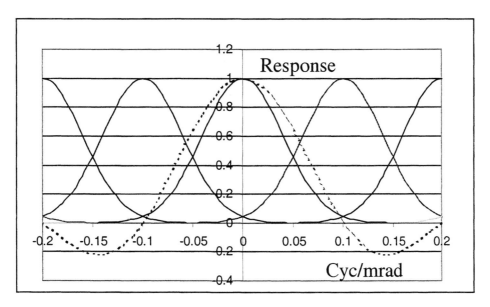

Figure 4.2 Replicated spectra from sampling the picture at top right of Figure 4.1. The dashed line shows the MTF of the display pixels used in the picture at bottom left of Figure 4.1.

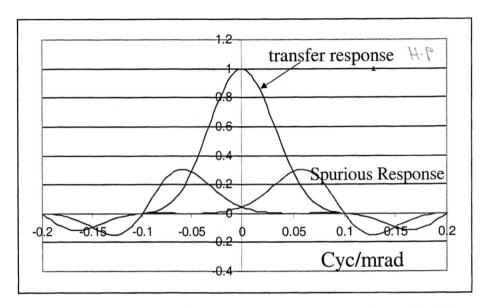

Figure 4.3 Transfer and spurious response for the picture shown at bottom left of Figure 4.1.

MTF twice as wide in frequency space. Therefore, the interpolation transfer function is extremely important, because it must remove the out-of-band spurious response.

Figure 4.4 shows the display MTF with half-sized pixels. The interpolation MTF is also shown. Details on the processing needed to create the interpolation MTF are provided later in this section. The post-sample MTF is the product of the display and interpolation MTFs. The new post-sample MTF has two good properties. First, the MTF is high in the baseband out to half the sample frequency, so the sensor transfer response is enhanced. Second, the new post-sample MTF filters out much of the spurious response beyond half the sample rate. As shown in the figure, the out-of-band spurious response is significantly reduced. The post-sample MTF controls the out-of-band spurious response to 0.32. The picture quality has improved as shown at the bottom right of Figure 4.1.

Notice that the interpolation MTF removes the sample generated replica spectra which was centered at the sample frequency (Figure 4.2). The replicated spectra at double the sample frequency remains. The interpolation MTF is periodic in frequency with a period twice the sample frequency; this is discussed below. The remaining spurious response at twice the sample frequency must be filtered by the display MTF and eye MTF. Another interpolation would reduce the replicated spectra at twice the sample rate, again improving the image.

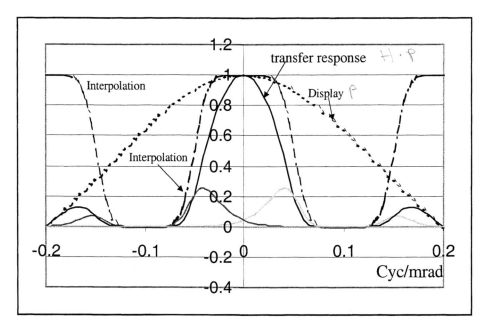

Figure 4.4 Figure shows the display MTF with half-sized pixels. The interpolation MTF is also shown. The post-sample MTF is the product of the display and interpolation MTFs. The out-of-band spurious response has been greatly reduced, and the resulting picture, seen at the bottom right of Figure 4.1, has improved image quality.

Conceptually, interpolation is accomplished by first reconstructing the image through the use of an interpolation function. In space, interpolation is the estimation of sampled image values at positions between given image samples. The Fourier transform of the interpolation function is taken as $Z(\xi)$. Envision $Z(\xi)$ as a temporary replacement for $P_{ix}(\xi)$. The interpolation function is chosen to pass the transfer response and filter out the spurious response. Once the image is completely reconstructed, it can be sampled at any spacing desired.

Obviously, interpolation cannot be used to remove any overlap between the transfer and spurious responses. Interpolation is used to remove the spurious response at frequencies above half the sample rate. However, in many practical circumstances, this tends to be the main contribution to the spurious response.

Interpolation functions which have a width of only a few samples and have the desired frequency characteristics can be generated by applying a smooth, Gaussian window to the sinc function. Some interpolation functions with good filtering characteristics are shown in Figure 4.5(a) through 4.5(c), and their frequency transforms are shown in Figure 4.6.

In concept, the interpolation function is convolved over the sample values resulting in a continuous output, and that output is re-sampled at more locations. In practice, knowing that the image is going to be re-sampled, only the new interpolated points need to be calculated.

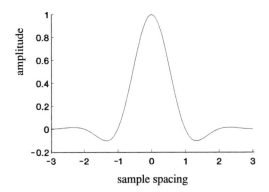

Figure 4.5(a) Six-sample-wide reconstruction function used to interpolate sampled data.

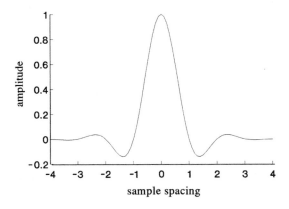

Figure 4.5(b)   Eight-sample-wide reconstruction function used to interpolate sampled data.

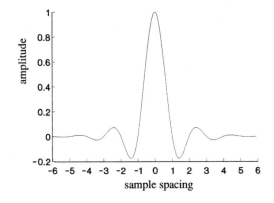

Figure 4.5(c)   Twelve-sample-wide reconstruction function used to interpolate sampled data.

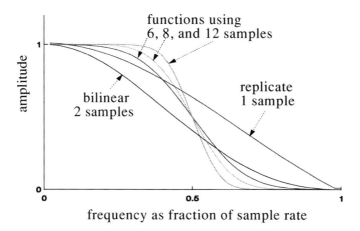

Figure 4.6 Filter characteristics for pixel replication, linear interpolation, and for reconstruction functions shown in Figures 4.5(a) through 4.5(c).

This is illustrated in Figure 4.7 for the six-sample-wide interpolation function. The interpolation function is centered at a point for which the interpolation is desired. Since the interpolation function is six samples wide, the three samples to each side of the interpolated point will contribute to the interpolated value. The coefficients which multiply each sample value are found by centering the interpolation function at the interpolated point and finding the amplitude of the function at the sample locations. For example, the interpolated value associated with the location halfway between samples 0 and 1

Value at 0.5 = 0.558 (value of sample 0 + value of sample 1)

- 0.088(value of sample -1 + value of sample 2)

+ 0.011(value of sample -2 + value of sample 3).

The interpolation points for the entire image can be found by convolving a discrete kernel over the image data. Some convolution coefficients for finding the midpoints between the image samples are shown in Table 4.1. These coefficients are based on the interpolation functions shown in Figures 4.5(a) through 4.5(c). Convolution kernels using these coefficients generate new data points and are used to double the size of an image.

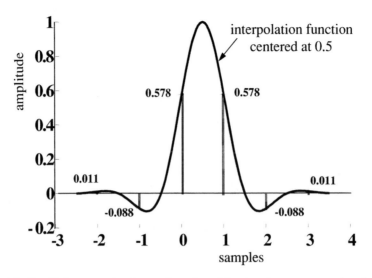

Figure 4.7 Coefficients used to interpolate the mid-points between samples. Interpolation function is centered at point for which interpolation is needed. The amplitude of the interpolation function at the adjacent sample locations gives the coefficients to use for interpolation. For example, to get the interpolated value for the 0.5 location, multiply 0.578 by the sum of the values for sample 0 and sample 1, subtract 0.088 multiplied by the values of samples -1 and 2, then add the product of 0.011 by the values of samples -2 and 3.

Table 4.1 Kernel coefficients applied to data on both sides of interpolation point.

Type/size	Kernel Coefficients					
linear	0.5					
6 samples	0.58	-.089	0.011			
8 samples	0.604	-0.13	0.032	-0.006		
12 samples	0.6213	-0.1704	0.0693	-0.0276	0.01	-0.003

As an example, the 6 sample wide interpolation will be used to double the size of an image [*Img*].

$$[Img] = \begin{bmatrix} Img11 & Img12 & Img13 & ... & ... & Img1N \\ Img21 & Img22 & Img23 & ... & ... & Img2N \\ ... & ... & ... & ... & ... & ... \\ ... & ... & ... & ... & ... & ... \\ ImgM1 & ImgM2 & ImgM3 & ... & ... & ImgMN \end{bmatrix}$$

An array [*Img'*] is generated with twice the image elements both horizontally and vertically (the final image contains four times as many display elements).

$$
[Img'] = \begin{array}{cccccccccc}
[Img11 & 0.0 & Img12 & 0.0 & Img13 & 0.0 & ... & ... & 0.0 & Img1N \\
0.0 & 0.0 & 0.0 & 0.0 & 0.0 & 0.0 & ... & ... & 0.0 & 0.0 \\
Img21 & 0.0 & Img22 & 0.0 & Img23 & 0.0 & ... & ... & 0.0 & Img2N \\
0.0 & 0.0 & 0.0 & 0.0 & 0.0 & 0.0 & ... & ... & 0.0 & 0.0 \\
... & ... & ... & ... & ... & ... & ... & ... & ... & ... \\
... & ... & ... & ... & ... & ... & ... & ... & ... & ... \\
... & ... & ... & ... & ... & ... & ... & ... & ... & ... \\
ImgM1 & 0.0 & ImgM2 & 0.0 & ImgM3 & 0.0 & ... & ... & 0.0 & ImgMN \\
0.0 & 0.0 & 0.0 & 0.0 & 0.0 & 0.0 & ... & ... & 0.0 & 0.0]
\end{array}
$$

For the 6 sample wide interpolation, the horizontal interpolation kernel is [*KH*] and the vertical kernel is [*KV*].

$[KH] = [0.011 \quad 0.0 \quad -0.089 \quad 0.0 \quad 0.58 \quad 1.0 \quad 0.58 \quad 0.0 \quad -0.089 \quad 0.0 \quad 0.011]$

$[KV] = [0.011 \quad 0.0 \quad -0.089 \quad 0.0 \quad 0.58 \quad 1.0 \quad 0.58 \quad 0.0 \quad -0.089 \quad 0.0 \quad 0.011]^T$

where T indicates the transpose of the array. The horizontal convolution is performed first in order to generate complete horizontal rows. After the horizontal convolution with [*KH*], the vertical convolution with [*KV*] is performed. After the vertical convolution, the matrix *Interp* contains the final, double-sized image.

$[Interp] = \{[Img'] * [KH]\} * [KV]$

where * means convolution.

The interpolation process should be thought of as performing a near-optimum reconstruction and then re-sampling at a higher frequency so that more display pixels are used in the final image. This technique can be used to increase the size of the displayed image, or it can be used with smaller display pixels to obtain a more optimum reconstruction of the image. In either case, interpolation techniques provide a way of estimating the shape of the pre-sampled image between sensor samples. If no interpolation is used, the shape of the image between samples depends upon the inherent shape of the display pixels. When interpolation is used, the inherent display pixel shape has less effect on the final image.

The response function for a sampled imager is now extended to include the interpolation function MTF. Based on Equation 3.7:

Transfer response $= Z(\xi)P_{ix}(\xi)H(\xi)$

Spurious response $= Z(\xi)P_{ix}(\xi)H(\xi-\nu)e^{-j\phi} + Z(\xi)P_{ix}(\xi)H(\xi+\nu)e^{j\phi}]$ (4.1)

However, the interpolation function MTF, $Z(\xi)$, is not one of the curves shown in Figure 4.6, because those curves do not include the effect of re-sampling. For example, the MTF shown for linear interpolation is $\mathrm{sinc}^2(\pi\xi X/2)$, where ξ is frequency in cycles per milliradian (for example) and X is the sample spacing in milliradians. This is the MTF associated with convolving a triangle over the sample points. This MTF is appropriate if many interpolated points are used between each of the original sample points. However, if a single, new mid-point value is interpolated between each original sample, then the effect of re-sampling on $Z(\xi)$ must be considered.

The MTF for discrete, linear interpolation can be found in the following manner. As discussed at the end of Chapter 1, the spatial distribution corresponding to the Fourier transform of the samples is a set of Dirac delta functions with areas equal to the sample values. Linear interpolation can be represented by a set of three delta functions which are convolved over the sample points to yield the interpolated image. One delta function is unity magnitude, the other two are one half value, offset to either side of the unity delta function by half a sample width.

New samples $= [\sum_n f(x)\delta(x-nX)]*[\delta(x)+0.5\delta(x-X/2)+0.5\delta(x+X/2)]$

    (4.2)

where $*$ means convolution.

A convolution in the spatial domain corresponds to a multiplication in the frequency domain. The Fourier transform associated with linear interpolation is the transform of the three delta functions. The Fourier transform of the three delta functions is multiplied by one half to normalize response to unity at zero frequency.

$$Z(\omega)_{linear} = 0.5[1+0.5e^{-i\omega X/2} +0.5e^{i\omega X/2}]$$
$$= 0.5+0.5\cos(\omega X/2).$$

    (4.3)

The MTF for the other interpolation functions can be found in a similar fashion.

$$Z(\omega)_{replicate} = \cos(\omega X / 4)$$

$$Z(\omega)_{k-samp} = 0.5 + \sum_{j=1}^{k/2} a(j)\cos[(2j-1)\omega X / 2]$$

(4.4)

where $a(j)$ are the coefficients shown in Table 4.1.

Figures 4.8(a) and (b) show the filtering characteristics of the discrete interpolation functions. The filtering functions in Figure 4.8(a) are cyclic (periodic) with a period double the original sample frequency. The replication MTF is periodic with a period four times the sample frequency.

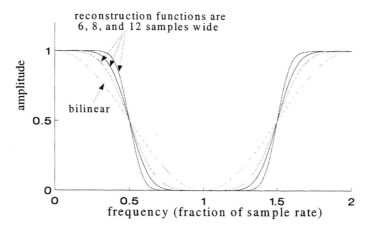

Figure 4.8(a) MTF of discrete interpolation functions. A good interpolation function removes the spurious response centered at the sampling frequency with minimum effect on the transfer response.

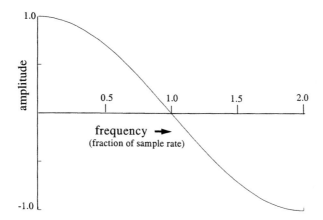

Figure 4.8(b) MTF associated with pixel replication. This filter function does not provide good rejection of the spurious response term that is centered at the sample frequency.

A good interpolation function will remove the first, replicated sideband in the original data, while not significantly degrading the transfer response of the system. Replication does a poor job of suppressing out-of-band spurious response and also has a degrading effect on the transfer response. Linear interpolation is much better than replication in terms of suppressing out-of-band spurious response. Linear interpolation does, however, degrade the transfer response. The 6, 8 or 12 sample wide interpolation functions do an excellent job of rejecting out-of-band spurious response while having very little degrading effect on the transfer response.

The picture shown in Figure 4.9 is a charge-coupled-device camera image of a pen and ink drawing of a helicopter. Figures 4.10, 4.11, and 4.12 show the helicopter enlarged eight times by using replication, bilinear interpolation, and the six-sample interpolation function, respectively.

The spurious response in the replicated image masks the underlying picture. The blocky images make it difficult for the visual system to integrate the picture information. Bilinear interpolation provides a much better image than pixel replication. When compared to the images created with bilinear interpolation, the images created with the broader, six-sample interpolation function are somewhat sharper and have fewer spurious artifacts.

Figure 4.9 CCD camera image of a pen and ink drawing of a helicopter.

4.2 CLASSICAL DESIGN CRITERIA FOR SAMPLED IMAGING SYSTEMS

There are four well-known criteria for the design of sampled imaging systems: Schade's, Legault's, Sequin's, and the Kell factor. These criteria are all based on a subjective assessment of image quality.

The Schade criterion requires that the transfer (baseband) response MTF be less than or equal to 0.15 at the half-sample rate of the sensor, as shown in Figure 4.13. The transfer MTF is the product of the pre-sample MTF and the post sample MTF. Schade suggests that these MTFs be equal, so that both pre- and post-sample MTFs should be 0.4 or less at the half-sample rate. In this case, sampling artifacts do not have a significant effect upon the imagery.

$$0.4 = MTF_{opt} \cdot MTF_{det}$$

Figure 4.10 Helicopter drawing magnified eight times by pixel replication.

Figure 4.11 Helicopter drawing magnified eight times by bilinear interpolation. Spurious artifacts are considerably reduced when compared with the pixel replication shown in Figure 4.10.

Figure 4.12   Helicopter drawing magnified eight times by using the six-sample interpolation function shown in Figure 4.5(a). Picture is sharper and has fewer spurious artifacts than pictures generated with pixel replication or bilinear interpolation.

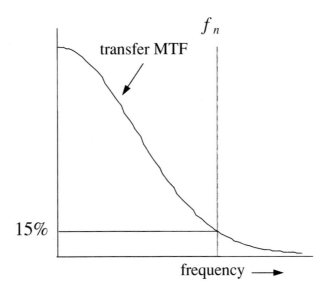

Figure 4.13 Schade's criterion is that the transfer response should be 15% or less at half the sample frequency f_n.

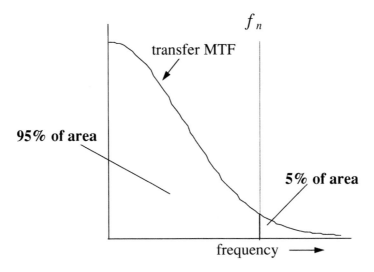

Figure 4.14 Legault's criterion is that 95% of the area under the transfer MTF curve should fall below the half-sample frequency f_n.

The Legault criterion requires that at least 95 percent of the area under the sensor's transfer response MTF curve be within the half-sample rate, as illustrated in Figure 4.14. The area under the MTF curve is integrated from zero frequency to the half sample frequency; the result should be at least 95% of the total area under the MTF curve. There is no guidance on the separation of pre-sample and post-sample MTF. An interesting note here is that, if a Gaussian pre-sample MTF and a Gaussian post-sample MTF are used, Legault's and Schade's criteria are identical.

For both the Schade and Legault formulations, the post-sample MTF includes only the physical display MTF; the eye MTF is not included. This means that the criteria are tied to unspecified viewing conditions. However, experiments with TV viewers established that viewers position themselves at a sufficient distance from the display that the display raster is not visible. That is, given a choice, the viewer minimizes the visible out-of-band spurious content. Assuming that the viewer positions himself such that his eye MTF removes the out-of-band spurious content, the Schade and Legault criteria can be considered as establishing a maximum in-band aliased content.

Sequin suggested that the maximum response frequency of a sensor system is the point where the aliased response equals one-half of the true response. See Figure 4.15. The Sequin criterion is more pessimistic than either the Schade or Legault criterion. The Sequin frequency (the point where the aliased signal is half of the real signal) is generally specified as a percentage of the half-sample rate.

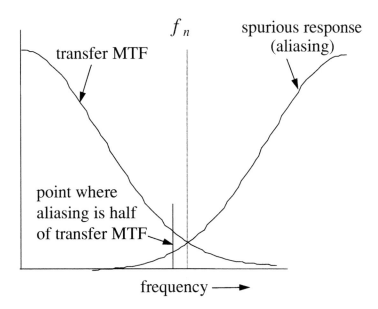

Figure 4.15 Sequin's criterion is that the sensor's frequency response is limited to the point on the frequency axis where the aliased response is half of the transfer response.

The Kell factor is commonly used when specifying television resolution. It suggests that sensor resolution in the vertical direction is limited to 70% of the number of lines. That is, because of the vertical raster, vertical resolution is limited to 35% of the sample frequency. A 1,000 line television would be credited with 700 lines of resolution or 350 line-pairs of resolution per picture height.

All of these criteria are subjective and are selected based on how pleasing the imagery is to the observer. None of these criteria are based on performance measurements using imagery that has been accurately characterized.

4.3 MINIMUM RESOLVABLE TEMPERATURE DIFFERENCE, MINIMUM RESOLVABLE CONTRAST, AND THE HALF-SAMPLE LIMIT

This section describes the most commonly used model for predicting human performance when using electro-optical imagers. The model currently incorporates a *half-sample limit* which is meant to account for the performance degradation due to sampling. This section describes the half-sample limit and explains why the resulting performance predictions are pessimistic.

Most present-day models use the *Johnson Criteria* to predict the range at which a human can detect, recognize, or identify a target when using a particular sensor and display. When sampled sensors came into serious consideration for major weapon systems in the late 1980's, a *half-sample limit* was incorporated into these models. It was understood that sampling would introduce artifacts into the sensor imagery, and the half-sample limit was a way to restrict the range performance credited to sampled imagers.

The two basic assumptions supporting the half-sample limit are simple. First, regardless of the sensor's MTF and noise characteristics, spatial frequencies beyond the half-sample frequency cannot be reproduced by the imager. This assumption certainly appears to be supported by the Sampling Theorem. Further, this assumption is much less pessimistic than either the Kell factor or the Sequin criteria.

The second assumption is that spatial frequencies up to the half-sample frequency will be reproduced by the sensor system. This assumption ignores aliasing. The sampling theorem states that sampling must occur at a rate more than twice the highest frequency present. The Sampling Theorem does not suggest that frequencies up to the half-sample rate are faithfully reproduced unless aliasing is prevented by a pre-filter.

The assumptions surrounding the half-sample limit appear to be optimistic. It might appear that the half-sample limit would underestimate the degradation caused by sampling artifacts. This is not the case. For sensitive staring imagers, the half-sample limit results in pessimistic performance predictions.

Unfortunately, the reasons for this pessimism lie within the Johnson model itself. In order to explain the failure of the half-sample limit, we must first describe the model in which it is applied.

In the 1950's, John Johnson performed the following experiment. Scale models of eight different vehicles and one soldier were placed against a bland background in the laboratory. Observers viewed the targets through image intensifiers, and they performed detection, recognition, and identification tasks. Bar charts with the same contrast as the scale targets were used to establish the limiting resolution of the sensors under the ambient light level conditions. By this means, the maximum number of resolvable cycles across the target was determined for each task.

It was found that the number of just-resolvable cycles across each target required to perform each task was within 25 percent of a fixed number of cycles. One cycle was needed for detection, four for recognition, and 6 cycles for identification. These cycle criteria are for a 50-percent success rate. Other experiments established how the probability of task performance changes depending on the number of cycles on target. That is, if 6 cycles provide a 50% chance of target identification, then 9 cycles provide a 80% chance of correctly accomplishing the task. In this manner, the ability of the observers to perform target discrimination tasks with the sensor was related to their ability to resolve bar patterns with the sensor.

Minimum resolvable contrast (MRC) for visible sensors and minimum resolvable temperature difference (MRTD or simply MRT) for thermal infrared sensors are measurements that establish how well bar patterns can be seen using the sensor. MRC applies to sensors which image reflected light, and MRT applies to thermal sensors which image emitted radiation.

Figure 4.16 illustrates how an MRT or MRC measurement is performed. Bar patterns of various sizes are viewed with the sensor. For each size of bar pattern, the bar contrast is increased until the pattern is visible, and this threshold contrast is noted. The bar contrast is then decreased until the bars disappear, and this smaller contrast is noted. The MRC or MRT measurement for that size bar pattern is the average of the contrasts where the bars appeared and disappeared. The MRC or MRT values are plotted versus spatial frequency, where the spatial frequency is defined as the inverse of the bar-space dimension.

Figure 4.17 shows how the MRC or MRT is used to predict range performance when using the sensor. The target is represented as a square of area equal to the target area. The target has an average contrast with its local background. The MRT or MRC plot of contrast versus frequency is used to find the highest bar pattern frequency which is visible for the target contrast value. Given a highest or limiting frequency, the number of "cycles on target" is calculated.

For example, assume that the square representing the target is one meter on edge, and the target is at a range of 1 kilometer. Then the target subtends 1 milliradian on edge at the sensor position. Assume also that the target contrast is 1.5 at the target, but that the atmosphere reduces the contrast to 1 C at the sensor aperture.

The highest frequency visible through the sensor for the 1 C contrast is determined to be 2 cycles per milliradian horizontally and 1 cycle per milliradian vertically. The sensor is said to resolve 2 cycles across the target horizontally (1 milliradian times 2 cycles per milliradian), and the sensor resolves 1 cycle across the target vertically. In the most modern version of the model, the geometric mean of the horizontal and vertical resolved cycles (1.414 in this case) is used to predict the probability of task performance.

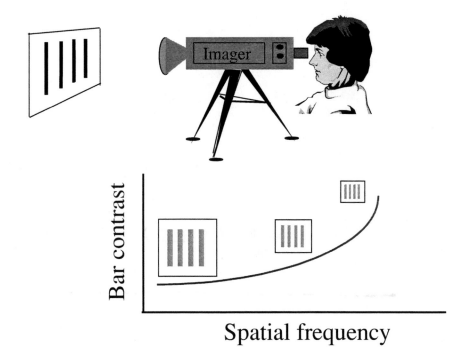

Figure 4.16 MRT or MRC measurement. For each size of bar pattern, the thermal (MRT) or luminance (MRC) contrast of the bars is varied until the pattern is just barely visible to the observer. The plot of threshold contrast versus spatial frequency (defined as inverse of bar spacing) is the MRT or MRC of the sensor system.

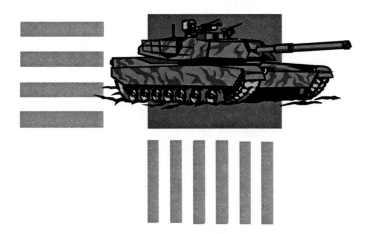

Figure 4.17 The Johnson Criteria. The target is represented as a square with the same total area as the target. The thermal (MRT) or luminance (MRC) contrast of the square is the average contrast of the target to its local background. The number of cycles that a sensor can resolve across this square determines how well the target can be detected, recognized, or identified.

Figure 4.18 shows MRT for a PtSi sensor and an InSb imager. Both sensors operate in the mid-wave infrared (MWIR), both have the same field of view, and both have 640 by 480 detector elements in the FPA. The PtSi sensor has $f/2.5$ optics and the detector integration time is 16 milliseconds. The InSb sensor has $f/3$ optics and the detector signal integration time is 1 millisecond. The InSb MRT is much better (much more sensitive) than the PtSi MRT because the InSb has much better quantum efficiency.

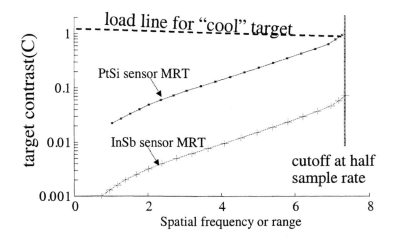

Figure 4.18 The MRTs for a PtSi and an InSb sensor are shown. These sensors have the same field of view and the same number of detectors in the FPA. Even though the InSb sensor has much better sensitivity, the two sensors are considered to have equal performance according to the "half-sample cutoff" rule.

Knowing the area of a target, A_t, plus the number of cycles, N, needed across the target to achieve a specified task performance, the frequency axis, ξ, in Figure 4.18 can be converted to range. The range, r, is

$$r = \xi \sqrt{A_t} / N .$$

The "load line for a cool target" shows the apparent contrast temperature of the target versus range. The point where the apparent target temperature crosses the sensor MRT defines the range at which the particular cycles across target criterion is met. Based on the MRTs shown in Figure 4.18, the InSb sensor should have much better range performance than the PtSi sensor.

However, the half-sample limit for these sensors is also shown in Figure 4.18. Since each sensor has the same field of view and the same number of detectors, the half-sample limit is the same for both sensors, and both sensors are predicted to have the same range performance. The half-sample limit makes little difference in predicting the performance of the less sensitive imager, but the more sensitive imager is not credited with additional range performance.

Even with the half-sample limit, the range performance predictions would be different if a colder target was considered. However, in practical terms, the thermal contrast used in Figure 4.18 is about as small as ever found in the field for normal targets.

The Johnson model with the half-sample limit is not a good design tool for sampled imagers. Experimentally, the InSb sensor performs much better under night conditions than the PtSi sensor. Further, the half-sample limit makes the model insensitive to changes in other major design parameters. For example, the model predicts no change in performance when using $F/7$ optics with the InSb sensor. However, we know from the experiments and field experience that the $F/3$ sensor is not performance limited by sampling artifacts even though some minor artifacts are visible. Also, we know that using a lens aperture less than half the size does significantly hurt performance. In the context of the Johnson model, the half-sample limit imposes an unreasonable constraint.

In the Johnson experiments, the limiting sensor resolution is a stand-in for the whole range of sensor characteristics. For example, a Gaussian blur can be defined by its 50% half-width, or its e^{-1} half width, or its $e^{-\pi}$ half width, or in many other ways. The $e^{-\pi}$ point on a Gaussian is just a way of defining the whole curve. In the absence of sampling, the limiting resolution of a sensor is a fairly good indicator of sensor bandwidth, sensor MTF characteristics, sensor noise levels, and other factors which affect performance.

In sampled imagers, sampling artifacts can affect performance. When using the Johnson model, the limiting resolution credited to a sampled sensor should be decreased to account for sampling artifacts. This is done in the MTF Squeeze model described in the next section. However, the limiting resolution to be used in the Johnson model is not dictated by the Sampling Theorem. In the Johnson model, the limiting resolution of the sensor is a measure of sensor "goodness." In sampled sensors, the limiting resolution used in the Johnson model can exceed the half-sample rate of the sensor.

4.4 MTF SQUEEZE

Two perception experiments were conducted at the Night Vision and Electronic Sensors Directorate (part of the U.S. Army Communication and Electronics Command) which quantify the relationship between the sampling artifacts generated by a sampled imager and target recognition and identification performance using that imager. The first experiment was a target recognition test and the second was a target identification test.

The recognition experiment involved a character recognition task. The application of character results to tactical vehicle recognition was verified by comparing the resulting theory to the results of previous experiments using tactical vehicles. (See *The Influence of Sampling on Target Recognition and Identification,* by Vollmerhausen et al.) The character recognition and tactical vehicle recognition tasks appear to require a similar, moderate level of visual discrimination.

The identification experiment used a target set with twelve tracked vehicles specifically chosen because they were easily confused. The test images included front, both sides, and rear aspects of the target taken at zero degrees elevation and eight different target aspects taken at 15 degrees elevation. This experiment involved high level visual discriminations.

Based on the data from these experiments, it was determined that the performance loss associated with sampling can be modeled as an increased blur on the imagery. The blur increase was characterized as a function of total spurious response for the recognition task and as a function of out-of-band spurious response for the identification task. Using the Fourier Similarity Theorem (see Goodman), an increase in blur is equivalent to a contraction of the modulation transfer function, thus *MTF Squeeze*. The squeeze for the recognition task is

$$SQ_{rec} = 1 - 0.32SR \qquad (4.5)$$

where *SR* is defined by Equation 3.8. The squeeze factor for the identification task is

$$SQ_{ID} = 1 - 2 * SR_{out-of-band} \qquad (4.6)$$

where $SR_{out-of-band}$ is defined by Equation 3.10.

Figure 4.19 illustrates the application of contraction or *MTF Squeeze* to the system MTF for the recognition task. The spurious response is calculated independently in the horizontal and vertical directions, and the squeeze factor given by Equations 4.5 (or 4.6 for identification) is calculated. At each (frequency, amplitude) point on the MTF curve, the frequency is scaled by the contraction factor. The contraction is applied separately to the horizontal and vertical MTF.

The results of these experiments show that in-band aliasing (aliasing which overlaps the baseband signal) did not degrade target identification performance, but out-of-band aliasing (such as visible display raster) degraded task performance significantly. Aliasing had less impact on the recognition task than the identification task, but both in-band and out-of-band aliasing degraded recognition performance to some extent.

Based on these experiments and other results reported in the literature, it appears that in-band aliasing has a strong effect on low level discrimination tasks like hot-spot detection; out-of-band aliasing has only a minor impact on these tasks. For high level discrimination tasks like target identification, however, out-of-band aliasing has a significant impact on performance, whereas in-band aliasing has a very minor effect. For intermediate-level discrimination tasks like target or character recognition, both in-band and out-of-band aliasing have a moderate impact on performance. The characteristics are summarized in Table 4.2.

Table 4.2 Performance dependence on spurious response.

TASK	In-Band *SR* (Edge shifting, line width variations, other local artifacts)	Out-of-Band *SR* (Raster, sharply demarcated pixels)	MTF squeeze
Hot-Spot Detection	Moderate to Large Dependence	Small Dependence	Speculation
Recognition	Moderate Dependence	Moderate Dependence	$1\text{-}0.32SR_{total}$
Identification	Small Dependence	Large Dependence	$1\text{-}2SR_{out\text{-}of\text{-}band}$

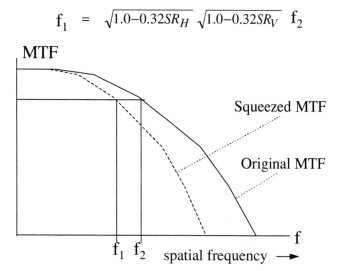

$$f_1 = \sqrt{1.0-0.32SR_H} \; \sqrt{1.0-0.32SR_V} \; f_2$$

Figure 4.19 Application of the MTF Squeeze. Contraction is calculated based on total spurious response ratio in each direction. Contraction of frequency axis is applied to both horizontal and vertical MTF. Contraction is applied to signal MTF, not the noise MTF.

In-band spurious response can be thought of as shifting object points, lines and edges; in-band aliasing can also modify the apparent width of an object or make the object disappear. That is, a fence post imaged by an undersampled sensor can be seen as wider, thinner, or slightly misplaced. In-band aliasing generates localized disturbances or artifacts in the image; in-band aliasing represents corruption of scene elements. Out-of-band spurious response is a pattern or artifact that is caused by the display. For example, raster on a CRT display or the sharp pixel edges on a low resolution flat panel display represent out-of-band spurious response.

High level discrimination tasks like target identification require many pixels on target. In-band aliasing causes small shifts in the position or intensity of minor target details, but these small corruptions do not affect the performance of high level tasks. However, in order to identify an object, the brain must integrate image information; out-of-band spurious response, like display raster, can mask image content.

For low level tasks like hot-spot detection, however, aliasing can cause the target to completely disappear at some sample phases; in-band aliasing can affect the performance of tasks that require only one or a few pixels on target. In these cases, out-of-band spurious response appears to have less impact on performance, perhaps because the observer need not integrate information over an extended area of the display.

The MTF Squeeze approach is an empirically-derived method for imposing a penalty for under sampling. The penalty is not as severe as the half-sample rate limit, but the MTF Squeeze method gives performance below that of a well-sampled imager with identical pre-sample and post-sample transfer functions.

4.5 SAMPLED IMAGER OPTIMIZATION

This section uses the MTF Squeeze model to evaluate sensor design. A sensitivity analysis is performed where various pre-sample blur and post-sample blur spots are considered in order to optimize the combination for target recognition and identification tasks. These results are compared to Schade's, Legault's, and Sequin's criteria, and suggestions are provided as guidance in sensor design. The important point here is that the MTF Squeeze approach is a valuable design tool for the optimization of sampled imaging systems

There are a number of historical design rules for sampled imaging systems including Schade's, Legault's and Sequin's criteria as presented in Section 4.2. These rules were based on a qualitative perception of image fidelity. The MTF Squeeze model determines the spurious response capacity of a sampled imaging system and increases the point spread function, or conversely decreases the Modulation Transfer Function, to account for the effects of sampling. Since acquisition (recognition and identification) performance with undersampled imagers is now quantified, we can use the model to optimize sampled imaging system design for these tasks.

The design of three different sampled imagers is optimized using the MTF Squeeze approach. The first is a sampled imaging system with a Gaussian pre-sample blur and a Gaussian post-sample reconstruction. This example is representative of a thermal imaging sensor system with a cathode-ray-tube display. The second system has a Gaussian pre-sample blur and a rectangular post-sample reconstruction. Such a system might represent an EO imager viewed on a flat panel display. The third system has a Gaussian pre-sample blur, a bilinear interpolation, and a rectangular post-sample reconstruction. This final example shows the importance of reconstruction processing when imagery is displayed using rectangular pixel elements.

Our design goal is to optimize the sensor systems for a range of intermediate and high-level visual tasks. The MTF Squeeze technique is used to optimize the sensor systems. The classical criteria for sampled imager design are also applied to the three examples in order to determine whether MTF Squeeze results are in consonance with the traditional standards.

4.5.1 Gaussian pre-sample blur and Gaussian post-sample blur

The MTF Squeeze approach is applied to a system with a Gaussian pre-sample blur and a Gaussian post-sample blur. Such a system is representative of thermal imaging systems with a CRT display. Note that, in this example, eye blur is included in the Gaussian post-sample blur. The pre-sample and post-sample Gaussian blur sizes are varied with respect to the sample spacing. The equation for the pre- and post-sample blurs is

$$h(x, y) = e^{-\pi(x/b)^2} e^{-\pi(y/b)^2} \tag{4.7}$$

where b is the scaling factor that generates a Gaussian spot with amplitude $e^{-\pi}$ at b. Since all blurs in this example are Gaussian, the blur size can be defined by giving the $e^{-\pi}$ half-width.

The scaling factor b is varied from 0.4 to 1.6 times the sample spacing for the pre-sample blur spot and from 0.4 to 2.0 times the sample spacing for the post-sample blur spot. This range represents physically realizable EO sensor systems. Remember that, in this example, the blurs are normalized to the sample spacing.

The transfer blur of the entire system is the convolution of the pre- and post-sample blurs. However, the *equivalent* blur of the system includes sampling artifacts and is found by applying the MTF Squeeze. The equivalent blur of the system is different for the recognition and identification tasks.

In the absence of sampling, the best system performance would occur with the least blur. Convolving a pre-sample blur of 0.4 and a reconstruction spot of 0.4 gives a system blur of 0.566. The total (in-band plus out-of-band) spurious response is 1.52, and this results in a recognition MTF squeeze of 0.51. These calculations are based on Equations 3.8 and 4.5. A contraction of 0.51 in frequency corresponds to a blur increase factor (recall the Fourier similarity theorem) of $1/0.51=1.94$ for an equivalent blur of 1.1 for recognition. The equivalent blur due to sampling degradation for recognition is almost double the actual blur. However, the system is certainly useful for the recognition task.

The out-of-band spurious response calculated with Equation 3.10 is 1.0. This out-of-band spurious response results in an unacceptable identification squeeze since, based on Equation 4.6, the squeeze factor is 0.0 and the resulting blur is infinite. A pre-sample blur of 0.4 with a post-sample reconstruction blur of 0.4 is not acceptable for identification.

Figure 4.20 shows equivalent blur for given pre- and post-sample Gaussian blurs. Figure 4.20(a) is for the identification task; Figure 4.20(b) is for the recognition task. In each figure, a different curve shows pre-blurs from 0.4 to 1.6 times the sample spacing. The post-sample blur is plotted on the abscissa and the equivalent blur resulting from the pre-blur and post-blur combination plus the effective increase in blur due to sampling is plotted on the ordinate. In Figure 4.20(b), using the curve for 0.4 pre-blur, the equivalent blur for 0.4 post-blur is 1.1 as stated above. Looking at Figure 4.20(a) for identification performance, the equivalent blur is off the scale.

For a system that is used for both recognition and identification, one reasonable design approach is to select the pre- and post-sample blurs that yield the least average effective blur for both tasks. Figure 4.20(c) shows equivalent blurs averaged for both tasks. Using the graph in Figure 4.20(c), the "averaged-blur" design gives a pre-sample blur of 0.6 times the sample spacing, a post-sample blur of 1.0 times the sample spacing, and an equivalent average blur of 1.7. These pre- and post-blurs result in an equivalent recognition blur of 1.5 and an equivalent identification blur of 1.9.

The MTFs for the MTF Squeeze optimized design are shown in Figure 4.21. The total transfer MTF shown in the figure is the product of the pre- and post-blur MTFs without squeeze. The recognition and identification squeezed MTFs are also shown.

Consider the historical design rules. Schade suggests that the transfer response be 15% at the half-sample rate, and Legault suggests that 95% of the area under the transfer MTF be at frequencies below the half-sample rate. It turns out that the Schade and Legault criteria are identical when the pre- and post-blurs are Gaussian. The Gaussian transfer response suggested by Schade and Legault criteria is shown in Figure 4.21. The Sequin cutoff frequency for the pre- and post-blurs resolution is 0.41 times the sample frequency (recall that this is the spatial frequency where the aliased response is half the transfer response).

These classical criteria should be compared to the actual transfer MTF of the MTF Squeeze design, not the squeezed MTF which is used to predict performance. It is readily apparent from Figure 4.21 that the MTF suggested by the MTF Squeeze method is much broader than the historical criteria would suggest. Remember also that the MTF Squeeze result includes the eye MTF whereas the Schade and Legault MTF curves do not. Including the eye MTF in the Schade and Legault curves would make the difference with the MTF Squeeze result even greater.

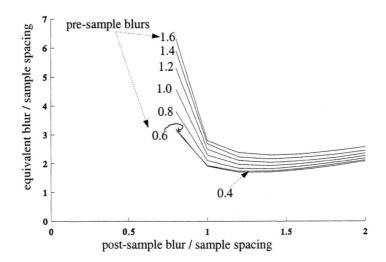

Figure 4.20(a) Effective blur as a function of pre- and post-sample blurs for the identification task. The abscissa gives the post-sample blur (to $e^{-\pi}$) and the ordinate gives the equivalent blur after the MTF Squeeze due to sample degradation. The various curves represent different pre-sample blur sizes.

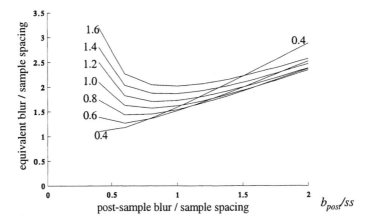

Figure 4.20(b) Effective blur as a function of pre- and post-sample blurs for the recognition task. The abscissa gives the post-sample blur (to $e^{-\pi}$) and the ordinate gives the equivalent blur after the MTF Squeeze due to sample degradation. The various curves represent different pre-sample blur sizes.

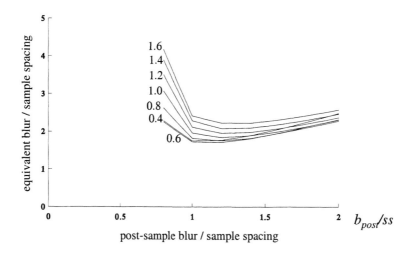

Figure 4.20(c) Effective blur as a function of pre- and post-sample blurs for the average blur for both identification and recognition tasks. The abscissa gives the post-sample blur (to $e^{-\pi}$) and the ordinate gives the equivalent blur after the MTF Squeeze due to sample degradation. The various curves represent different pre-sample blur sizes.

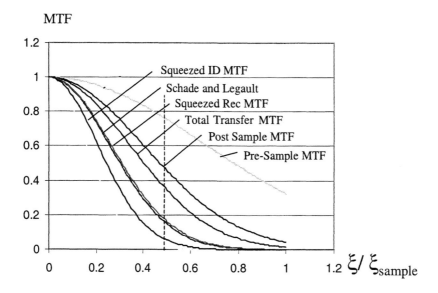

Figure 4.21 MTFs for the best Gaussian-Gaussian design. The Total Transfer MTF is the product of the pre-blur and post-blur MTFs. The MTFs shown for Sequin, Schade and Legault are based on generating pre-and post-blurs which meet their individual criterion. For example, the pre- and post-blurs for Schade and Legault have 40% MTF at the half-sample rate. The MTF Squeeze result suggests that the system is optimized with less blur than suggested by Schade, Legault or Sequin.

The task-oriented MTF Squeeze method suggests that the system should have less blur and can permit more sampling artifacts than the classical image quality criteria would suggest.

Also shown in Figure 4.21 are the squeezed system transfer functions for both the recognition and identification tasks. Note two interesting points. First, the cutoffs for both the recognition and identification transfer functions are beyond the half-sample rate of the system. That is, the system performance is not limited by the half-sample rate as would be suggested by the Johnson criteria.

Second, the equivalent blur for identification performance is greater than the blur for recognition performance (the MTF is squeezed more for identification than for recognition). This suggests an alternative design approach. Rather than minimizing the average, equivalent blurs for recognition and identification, select the pre-and post-blurs which yield equal equivalent blurs for recognition and identification.

With Gaussian blurs, reducing out-of-band spurious response leads to a reduction of the transfer response. Since out-of-band spurious response does not strongly affect recognition performance, increasing post-sample blur (from say 1.0 to 1.2) will degrade recognition performance. For recognition, the decreased performance due to reduced transfer response dominates over the increase in performance due to reduced spurious response. However, identification performance is helped significantly by decreasing out-of-band spurious response, so increasing the post-sample blur to 1.2 improves identification performance.

A small effective blur that is equivalent for both identification and recognition occurs with a pre-sample blur of 0.6 times the sample spacing and a post-sample blur of 1.2 times the sample spacing. These parameters give an equivalent blur of 1.7 for both the recognition and identification tasks. In this example, selecting equal blurs resulted in almost the same average blur as minimizing the average equivalent blur. As can be seen in Figure 4.20(c), the equivalent blur is almost constant in the post-blur range of 1.0 to 1.2 for a pre-blur of 0.6.

It is unfortunate that the effect of sampling on task performance depends on the nature of the sampling artifacts and on the task to be performed. The result is that system optimization is task dependent. In this example, the "optimum" design depends on how important the identification task is relative to the recognition task.

It should be noted, however, that we did not use the interpolation techniques described in Section 4.1 in this first example. The post-sample MTF was limited to a Gaussian shape. It is possible, in theory at least, to completely remove all of the out-of-band spurious response through digital processing and using a display with a lot of pixels. If an interpolation function like one of those listed in Table 4.1 [with the MTF shown in Figure 4.8(a)] is used, then the out-of-band response can be removed without seriously hurting the transfer response. For a given pre-blur and sample rate, removing all of the out-of-band spurious response will optimize the identification task. Any additional post-blur to remove in-band aliasing can then be based solely on optimizing the recognition task. Flexibility in digital processing and display design can greatly facilitate system optimization.

4.5.2 Gaussian pre-sample blur and rectangular post-sample blur

The previous system represented a thermal imaging system with a cathode-ray-tube display; many new and future systems will incorporate flat panel displays. The benefits are that the display is lightweight and conserves space. The disadvantage of such displays is that they often have sharply demarcated display pixel elements which generate large amounts of spurious response.

In the previous example, it was assumed that the Gaussian post-sample blur included the eye; in that example, a large number of individual post-sample blurs convolved to form an overall Gaussian post-sample blur. In this next example, the rectangular post-sample blur must be explicitly limited by the eye MTF, since otherwise the spurious response would be so large that identification could not be accomplished.

The eye MTF is comprised of pupil, retina, and tremor transfer functions

$$H_{eye}(\xi) = H_{pupil}(\xi)H_{retina}(\xi)H_{tremor}(\xi) \tag{4.8}$$

where ξ is the spatial frequency (cycles per milliradian to the eye). In this example, two eyes view the display, and the display luminance is 10 milliLamberts (10.7 footLamberts). The eye MTF using the data in Overington's *Vision and Acquisition* is

$$H_{eye}(\xi) = e^{-1.3\xi^{0.762}} e^{-0.375\xi^{1.21}} e^{-0.444\xi^2}. \tag{4.9}$$

The Gaussian pre-blur is given by Equation 4.7. The display element is assumed to be rectangular with a transfer function of

$$H_{disp}(\xi) = \text{sinc}(\pi ss\xi) \tag{4.10}$$

where ss is the sample spacing. We assume a 100 percent display fill factor.

With the completely Gaussian transfer response used in the last example, the $e^{-\pi}$ cutoff at blur radius b corresponded to $e^{-\pi}$ MTF cutoff at frequency $1/b$. In the current example, the equivalent blur radius is defined as the inverse of the $e^{-\pi}$ point on the MTF curve; that is, the blur radius is defined as the inverse of the frequency at which the MTF is 0.043. Again, the equivalent blur is normalized to sample spacing. In this example, the display pixel size and the sample spacing are the same, because a 100% fill factor is assumed. Sample spacing is expressed as the angular distance between samples to the eye in milliradians.

Pre-blur is varied from 0.4 to 1.8 sample spacings. Figure 4.22(a) shows the equivalent blur for identification. Figure 4.22(b) shows the equivalent blur for recognition. The abscissa in Figure 4.22 is sample spacing at the eye in milliradians rather than post-sample blur as in Figure 4.20. Sample spacing at the eye is important in this example because of the eye's MTF response. Also, since the display pixel fills the distance between samples, sample spacing at the eye also defines display pixel size. The sample spacing at the eye is changed by either varying viewing distance between eye and display or by varying the size of the display pixel.

The best results for recognition occur for a pre-blur of 0.8 and a sample spacing of 4 milliradians. A pre-blur larger than the minimum 0.4 is necessary in order to avoid excessive in-band aliasing. The large display pixel (small viewing distance) optimizes recognition by making the image large. Moving the eye closer to the display improves the transfer response of the system because the eye MTF becomes less important. The increased out-of-band spurious response which results from viewing the square display pixels up close is not particularly important for the recognition task.

Identification is best with a pre-blur of 0.4 and a 1 milliradian sample spacing at the eye. Identification is optimized by a small pre-blur because in-band aliasing does not affect the task, and the small pre-blur improves the transfer response. However, the square display pixels must be kept some distance from the eye in order to avoid the out-of-band spurious response which strongly degrades the identification task. For the identification task, viewing distance (or, alternatively, display size) is a compromise between a small, hard to see picture, or excessive out-of-band spurious response.

When the system is designed using the average equivalent blur, the optimum design calls for a pre-sample blur of 0.6 times the sample spacing and an angular sample spacing of 2 milliradians. For this combination of pre- and post-blurs, the equivalent identification blur is 2.0 and the equivalent recognition blur is 1.8.

The sample-replicated spectrum and post-sample (display and eye MTF) for this design are shown in Figure 4.23. Figure 4.24 shows the resulting transfer and spurious responses. Notice that the spurious response is in two parts because the replicas adjacent to the baseband are wide enough to cross the amplitude axis.

The baseband comes very near to Schade's criterion with an amplitude of 0.13 at the half-sample frequency. Legault's criterion is nearly satisfied with 94 percent of the baseband area below the half-sample rate. However, the transfer and spurious responses in Figure 4.24 include the eye MTF, whereas the Schade and Legault criteria consider only the sensor (camera) and display blurs. The transfer response would be significantly larger at the half-sample rate if the eye MTF was not included. Once again, the MTF Squeeze criteria suggests an optimum system which has less blur and permits more sampling artifacts than the classical sampling standards.

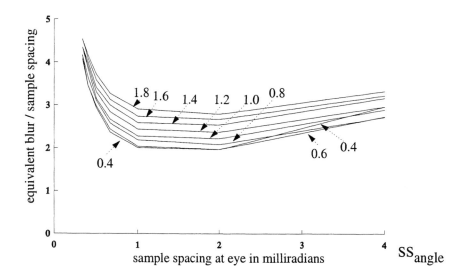

Figure 4.22(a)   Equivalent blur for the Gaussian pre-sample blur, rectangular display blur, and eye blur. This graph shows the identification equivalent blurs. The abscissa is sample spacing in milliradians at the eye. The numbers (0.4, 0.6,…,1.8) are the pre-sample blur normalized to sample spacing.

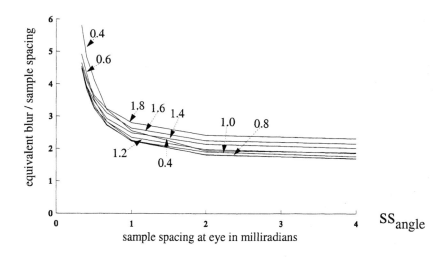

Figure 4.22(b)   Equivalent blur for the Gaussian pre-sample blur, rectangular display blur and eye blur. This graph shows the recognition equivalent blurs. The abscissa is sample spacing in milliradians at the eye. The numbers give the pre-sample blur radius normalized to sample spacing.

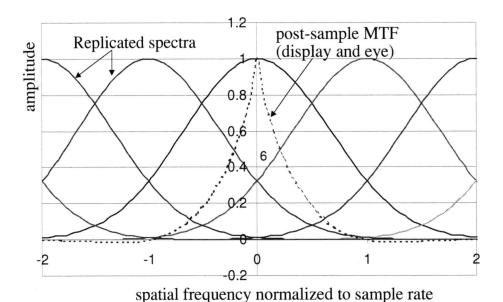

Figure 4.23 MTFs associated with second example. Pre-sample MTF replicated due to sampling. The post-sample MTF is also shown; the post-sample MTF includes eye MTF and rectangular pixel MTF.

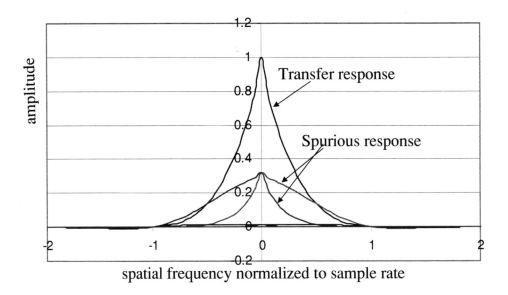

Figure 4.24 Transfer response (baseband MTF) and spurious components. Two spurious responses are shown because the replica from the negative frequency axis crosses to the positive side and vice-versa.

4.5.3 Optimizing the display of a 256 by 256 staring array imager

This third example illustrates how display technique can influence sensor performance. A sampled-imager design is described, and the effect of display interpolation is analyzed.

The sensor in this example uses a 256 by 256 pixel staring FPA. Diffraction wavelength is 4 micrometers. The effective focal length of the optics is 5 centimeters and the optical F-number is 2.5. The detector element pitch is 50 micrometers and the fill factor is 100%. The sensor field of view is 14.67 degrees full angle. The sensor instantaneous field of view is 1 milliradian, and the sensor sample rate is 1 sample per milliradian.

A 6 inch high by 6 inch wide flat panel display is used; viewing distance is assumed to be 12 inches. The display luminance is 10 footLamberts and the eye MTF is given by Equation 4.9. Display field of view at the eye is 28.07 degrees, and system magnification is therefore 1.91. The display has 512 by 512 pixels. The intensity pattern of a single display pixel is shown in Figure 4.25. The pixels are essentially square but with softened edges. The intensity distribution resulted from convolving a square pixel with a Gaussian with half-width (to $e^{-\pi}$) of 10 percent of the pixel width. Each sensor sample subtends 0.5 milliradians in space and 0.96 milliradians at the eye.

The MTFs associated with the sensor and display are shown in Figure 4.26. The optics are diffraction limited, and the pre-sample MTF is the product of the optics and detector MTFs shown in the figure. The display MTF shown in Figure 4.26 is quite broad relative to the detector MTF because the display pixel subtends half the angle.

The interpolation MTFs used in this example are shown in Figure 4.8. Several post-sample (reconstruction) MTFs are created by multiplying each MTF in Figure 4.8 by the display pixel MTF shown in Figure 4.26. For each interpolation MTF, the total and out-of-band spurious responses are calculated using Equations 3.8 and 3.10, respectively. The resulting recognition and identification MTF Squeezes are found using Equations 4.5 and 4.6. The various interpolation MTFs affect the transfer response to a slight degree; the integrated area under the transfer response is shown in the first row of Table 4.3.

Table 4.3 shows how recognition and identification performance varies with the selected interpolation technique. The results for pixel replication also apply to a 256 by 256 element display where the display pixels are larger so that the display size is still 6 inch on a side. The relative range performance indicated in the table is based on the MTF Squeeze factors with a minor adjustment for the variation in the transfer response. The relative range performance is normalized to the range performance when using pixel replication (or using a display with 256 by 256 pixels).

Table 4.3 Influence of interpolation technique on task performance. Range is given in kilometers.

	Replicate	Bilinear	6-sample	8-sample	12-sample
transfer rsp	0.31	0.28	0.296	0.3	0.303
SR_{total}	0.454	0.34	0.302	0.292	0.285
Rec. MTF Sq.	0.855	0.891	0.903	0.907	0.909
Rec. range	**1.0**	**0.925**	**1.0**	**1.02**	**1.04**
$SR_{out\text{-}of\text{-}band}$	0.23	0.126	0.0756	0.0586	0.043
ID MTF Sq.	0.54	0.748	0.849	0.883	0.914
ID range	**1.0**	**1.2**	**1.48**	**1.57**	**1.65**

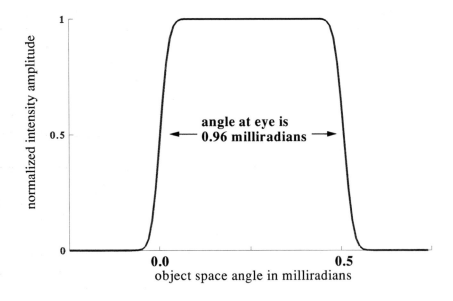

Figure 4.25 Intensity distribution from single display pixel used in third example. The pixel is essentially square but has soft edges. The 50% amplitude full-width of the pixel is 0.5 milliradians in object space. System magnification is 1.91, so that each pixel subtends 0.96 milliradian at the eye.

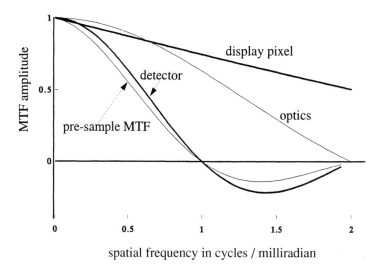

Figure 4.26 MTFs associated with the sensor in third example. The display pixel MTF is quite broad because the pixels are small; there are twice as many display pixels as sensor samples both horizontally and vertically.

The recognition performance varies very little for the various interpolation techniques. The decrease in recognition performance with bilinear interpolation is due to the reduced transfer response caused by the bilinear MTF. Although the bilinear interpolation significantly reduces spurious response, the recognition performance is not greatly affected by the spurious response.

Identification performance varies greatly with choice of interpolation technique; range performance can be improved by as much as 65% by using a 12-sample wide interpolation kernel. Bilinear interpolation provides a 20% range improvement.

Recognition performance involves tasks like reading characters or telling a car from a truck. Identification tasks involve correctly labeling the type of car. It has been observed by pilots flying night vision systems that raster in the image can make finding the airfield very difficult. Finding the airfield is apparently an "identification" task because it involves visually integrating information over some extended region of the display. These "identification-like" tasks are seriously affected by out-of-band spurious response. Fortunately, the out-of-band spurious response can be removed by display processing; the sensor need not be improved.

Dither and dynamic sampling are described in later chapters. If we assume that the application of one of these techniques can remove all of the sampling artifacts, then recognition range performance (normalized to the pixel replicate performance given in Table 4.3) would be 1.17, and the relative identification performance range would be 1.85. Compare these results to the 1.04 recognition range and 1.65 identification range obtained with the 12-sample interpolation. In this example, most of the performance gain can be achieved with display processing alone.

BIBLIOGRAPHY

Arguello, R., H. Kessler, and H. Sellner, "Effect of Sampling, Optical Transfer Function Shape, and Anisotropy on Subjective Image Quality," SPIE Vol. 310 Image Quality, 1981.

Barbe, D. and S. Campana, "Imaging Arrays Using the Charge Coupled Concept," In Advances in Image Pickup and Display (B. Kazan, Ed.), Vol. 3, pp. 171-296, 1977.

D'Agostino, J., M. Friedman, R. LaFollette, and M. Crenshaw, "An Experimental Study of the Effects of Sampling on FLIR Performance," Proceedings of the IRIS Specialty Group on Passive Sensors, Infrared Information Analysis Center, ERIM, Ann Arbor, MI, 1990.

Flynn, D., and B. Sieglinger, "Formalism for Analyzing Spatial, Spectral, and Temporal Effects in a Hardware-in-the-Loop System Involving a Pixelized Projector and a Passive Imaging Sensor," SPIE Vol. 2741, p. 46, 1996.

Goodman, J., *Fourier Optics*, McGraw-Hill, San Francisco, CA, p. 9, 1968.

Holst, G., "Effects of Phasing on MRT Target Visibility," SPIE Vol 1488, Infrared Imaging Systems: Design, Analysis, Modeling, and Testing II, p. 90, 1991.

Howe, J., In Electro-Optical Systems Design, Analysis, and Testing, "Electro-Optical Imaging System Performance Prediction," (Dudzik, Ed.), The IR & EO systems Handbook, Vol. 4, p. 92, ERIM IIAC, Ann Arbor, MI, and SPIE, Bellingham, WA, 1993.

Howe, J., L. Scott, S. Pletz, J. Horger, and J. Mark, "Thermal Model Improvement Through Perception Testing," Proceedings of the IRIS Specialty Group on Passive Sensors, Infrared Information Analysis Center, ERIM, Ann Arbor, MI, 1989.

Huck, F., S. Park, D. Speray, and N. Halyo, "Information Density and Efficiency of Two-Dimensional Sampled Imagery, SPIE Vol. 310, p. 36, 1981.

Kruthers, L., T. Williams, G. O'Brien, K. Le, and J. Howe, "A Study of the Effects of Focal Plane Array Design Parameters on ATR Performance," SPIE Vol 1957, p. 165, 1993.

Legault, R., "The Aliasing Problems in Two-Dimensional Sampled Imagery," In Perception of Displayed Information, (L. Biberman, Ed.), pp. 279-312, Plenum, New York, 1973.

Lloyd, J., Thermal Imaging Systems, Plenum Press, New York, p. 184, 1975.

Meitzler, T., T. Cook, G. Gerhart, and R. Freeling, "Spatial Aliasing Effects in Ground Vehicle IR Imagery," SPIE Infrared Imaging Systems, Vol. 1689, pp. 226-241, 1992.

Overington, I., Vision and Acquisition, Pentech Press, London, 1976.

Owen, P. and J. Dawson, "Resolving the Differences in Oversampled and Undersampled Imaging Sensors: Updated Target Acquisition Modeling Strategies for Staring and Scanning FLIR Systems," SPIE Vol. 1689, pp. 251-261, 1992.

Park. S., and R. Hazra, "Aliasing as Noise: A Quantitative and Qualitative Assessment," SPIE Vol. 1969, pp. 54-65, 1993.

Park, S., and R. Schowengerdt, "Image Sampling, Reconstruction, and the Effect of Sample-Scene Phasing," Applied Optics, Vol. 21, No. 17, p. 3142, 1982.

Reichenbach, S., and S. Park, "Small Convolution Kernels for High-Fidelity Image Restoration," IEEE Transactions on Signal Processing, Vol. 39, No. 10, pp. 2263-2274, 1991.

Reichenbach, S., S. Park, G. O'Brien, and J. Howe, "Efficient, High-Resolution Digital Filters for FLIR Images," SPIE Vol. 1705, pp. 165-176, 1992.

Schade, O., "Image Reproduction by a Line Raster Process," In *Perception of Displayed Information*, (L. Biberman, Ed.), pp. 233-277, Plenum, New York, 1973.

Schade, O., "Image Gradation, Graininess, and Sharpness in Television and Motion-Picture Systems," J. SMPTE, 1953, 61, pp. 97-164.

Sequin, C., IEEE Transactions, Vol. 20, p. 535, 1973.

Tannas, L., Flat-Panel Displays and CRTs, pp. 19 & 39, Van Nostrand Reinhold Co., New York, 1985.

Vollmerhausen, R., "Display of Sampled Imagery," IRIA-IRIS Proceedings: Meeting of the IRIS Specialty Group on Passive Sensors, Vol. 1, pp. 175-192, 1990.

Vollmerhausen, R., "Impact of Display Modulation Transfer Function on the Quality of Sampled Imagery," SPIE Aerospace/Defense Sensing and Controls, Vol. 2743, pp. 12-22, 1996.

Vollmerhausen, R., R. Driggers, and B. O'Kane "The Influence of Sampling on Recognition and Identification Performance," Optical Engineering, Vol. 36, No. 5, 1999.

Vollmerhausen, R., R. Driggers, and B. O'Kane, "The Influence of Sampling on Target Recognition and Identification," Optical Engineering, Vol. 38, No. 5, 1999.

Vollmerhausen, R., R. Driggers, C. Webb and T. Edwards, "Staring Imager Minimum Resolvable Temperature (MRT) Measurements Beyond The Sensor Half Sample Rate," Optical Engineering, Vol. 37, No. 6, p. 1763, Jan, 1998.

Vollmerhausen, R., and R. Driggers, "NVTHERM: Next Generation Night Vision Thermal Model," 1999 IRIS Passive Sensors Proceedings, 440000-121-X(1), Vol. 1, pp.121-134, IRIA Center, ERIM, Ann Arbor, MI.

Vollmerhausen, R., and R. Driggers, "Modeling the Target Acquisition Performance of Staring Array Sensors," 1998 IRIS Passive Sensors Proceedings, 440000-82-X(1), Vol. 1, pp. 211-224, IRIA Center, ERIM, Ann Arbor, MI.

Webb, C., "Dynamic Minimum Resolvable Temperature Difference for Staring Focal Plane Arrays," Proceedings of the IRIS Specialty Group on Passive Sensors, Infrared Information Analysis Center, ERIM, Ann Arbor, MI, 1993.

Webb, C., "Results of Laboratory Evaluation of Staring Arrays," SPIE Vol. 1309, Infrared Imaging Systems: Design, Analysis, Modeling, and Testing, p. 271, 1990.

Wittenstein, W., "The MTDP – A New Approach to Assess Undersampled Thermal Imagers," Optical Engineering, Vol. 38, No. 5, 1999.

Wittenstein, W., W. Fick, and U. Raidt, "Range Performance of Two Staring Imagers - Presentation of the Field Trial and Data Analysis," SPIE Vol. 2743, p. 132, 1996.

Wittenstein, W., F. Fontanella, A. Newberry, and J. Baars, "The Definition and the OTF and the Measurement of Aliasing for Sampled Imaging Systems," Optica Acta, Vol. 29, No. 1, p. 46, 1982.

5

INTERLACE AND DITHER

Interlace and dither reduce sensor sampling intervals without increasing detector count. A high-resolution frame image is comprised of two or more lower resolution fields or sub-images taken sequentially in time. Between each field or sub-image, a nodding mirror or other mechanical means is used to move the locations where the scene is sampled. Interlace and dither achieve high resolution while minimizing focal plane array complexity.

The mechanical operation of a dither or microscan mirror is illustrated in Figure 5.1. A mirror is inserted between the objective lens and the FPA. The angular motion of the mirror about the scan axis is very small. Image translation on the FPA is sub-pixel (that is, less than a sample spacing). The figure indicates a horizontal translation of the image, but the mirror can be made to scan about any axis. The sub-pixel image translation provided by the scan mirror allows changing the sample phase of the FPA relative to the scene.

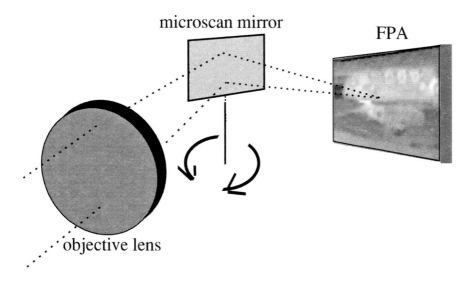

Figure 5.1 Operation of microscan mirror. Mirror permits changing sample phase by sub-pixel translation of image relative to the FPA.

Interlace generally has the connotation that the sub-images or field images are taken and displayed in time synchronism. That is, the pixels from sub-images taken at different times are not combined and then displayed, but rather the time sequencing of the sensor field images is maintained at the display. The reduced resolution, field images are combined into a high resolution image by the human visual system. *Dither*, on the other hand, generally has the connotation that the field images are combined to form a higher resolution image prior to the display.

Interlace is used to improve sensor sampling without increasing pixel rate or electronic throughput of the system. Interlace takes advantage of the eye's ability to integrate multiple fields of imagery, presented in time sequence, into a higher resolution frame.

Video display rates must be 50 or 60 Hertz in order to avoid perceptible flicker, but each 50 or 60 Hertz image need not display every pixel. Flicker is avoided in most circumstances by displaying every-other pixel in each field. Flicker can occur when the image contains lines which are one pixel wide as in graphic plots. In that case, local regions of the image do not have approximately the same intensity between fields. Most natural scenes, however, do not contain such constructs, and the sensor pre-sample blur mitigates the problem when it does occur.

Standard video uses two fields per frame and vertical interlace. That is, the video display is a vertical raster of lines, and every-other line is displayed in every-other field. In the United States, the field rate is 60 Hertz and the frame rate is 30 Hertz. In Europe, the standard rate is 50 Hertz field and 25 Hertz frame. In this chapter, the U.S. standard is assumed.

Figure 5.2 illustrates video interlace. Each 1/60th of a second, an interlaced sensor gathers every-other horizontal row of scene samples. The video display shows every-other horizontal line. Every-other video line is collected by the sensor in each field. Every-other video line is displayed during each field. Interlace is used because the full resolution image need only be produced and displayed 30 times a second.

With an interlaced sensor and display, the human visual system integrates the full resolution image whether the image is stationary or moving relative to the sensor. The 30 Hertz update of pixel information is more than adequate to support the perception of smooth apparent motion. Exceptions to smooth apparent motion can occur. If the scene is comprised of very simple, high contrast structures, then image breakup can sometimes be seen during scene-to-sensor motion. However, for natural, complex scenes, such breakup is very rare. For a human observer, interlace provides full resolution imagery at half the pixel throughput.

The terms *dither* or *microscanning* are generally only applied to staring imagers. Although vertical interlace can certainly be accommodated by a staring imager, it is also common for the field sub-images to be combined into a high resolution image prior to the display. Figure 5.3 illustrates diagonal dither. At the top of the figure, imagery is collected by the low-resolution FPA. A mirror is used to move the scene diagonally across the FPA, so that the sample locations are changed. A second sub-image is then collected. The two sub-images are combined in the electronics to form a higher resolution image which is then displayed. Combining the high resolution image prior to the display gives more flexibility in the dither sampling pattern. Extra samples can be added horizontally or diagonally as well as vertically, and the standard video display is still used. Combining pixels from fields taken at different times, however, can lead to artifacts in the displayed imagery when there is scene-to-sensor motion.

The sampling advantages of interlace and dither are described in the next section. The sampling advantages are described for a static scene; there is no scene-to-sensor motion. The subsequent section describes the impact of dither on sensor resolution and sensitivity. The final section of this chapter describes the effect of motion.

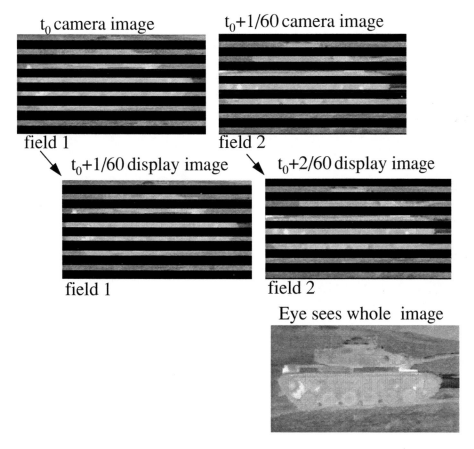

Figure 5.2 Illustration of interlace. At top, the sensor or camera collects the first field of imagery consisting of alternate horizontal lines. The first field is displayed 1/60th of a second later. The camera then collects the lines not collected in the first field and these are subsequently displayed.

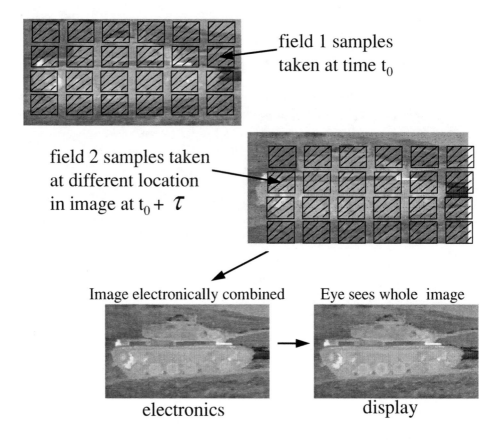

Figure 5.3   Illustration of dither. At top, imagery is collected by a focal plane array. The scene is moved slightly across the array by a nodding mirror. Some time τ later, imagery is collected at different sample locations. The combined samples from the two fields or sub-images are electronically combined to form a higher resolution image which is subsequently displayed

5.1 SAMPLING IMPROVEMENT WITH STATIC SCENE

An FPA sampling grid is shown in Figure 5.4. The sampling grid shown is a rectangular array of points. For these examples, the sample spacing is taken as 1 milliradian. Common interlace and dither geometries are shown in Figures 5.5 through 5.7.

Figure 5.5 shows vertical dither or interlace. The first field or sub-image collects samples at the locations shown by the black dots. At some time τ later, the field 2 samples are taken at the locations of the gray dots. Vertical dither adds vertical samples while the horizontal sample rate remains the same as in Figure 5.4.

Figure 5.6 shows two of several ways of dithering both horizontally and vertically. Sub-image 1 is collected by the FPA with the microscan mirror

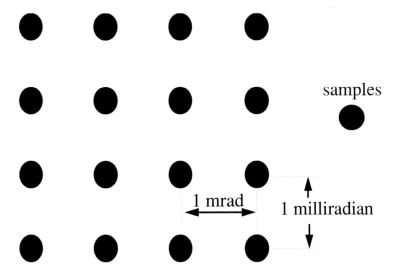

Figure 5.4 Sampling grid for each field or sub-image. The example sample spacing is 1 milliradian.

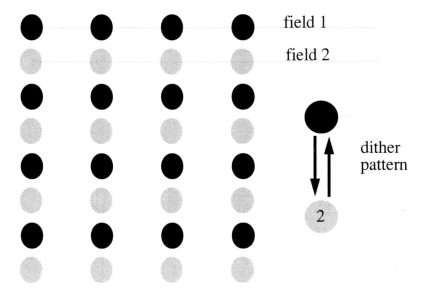

Figure 5.5 Vertical interlace or dither pattern adds extra vertical samples. The samples at black dot locations are taken during field 1. The samples at locations of gray dots are taken during field 2. The horizontal sample spacing is still 1 milliradian, but the vertical sample spacing is now 0.5 milliradians.

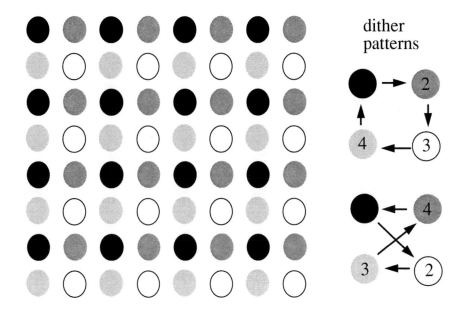

Figure 5.6 Scene is dithered both horizontally and vertically. The black, gray, light gray, and white dots represent samples taken during different fields. Sample spacing when all of the sub-images are combined is 0.5 milliradian both horizontally and vertically. The dither can be accomplished in multiple ways, only two of them shown. If the scene is static, then all of the dither patterns provide the same result.

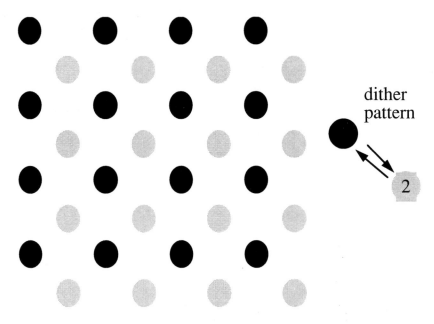

Figure 5.7 Diagonal dither. Black dots show sample locations during field 1. Gray dots show sample locations during field 2. Scene sampling has improved but neither horizontal nor vertical sampling is doubled.

stationary. The microscan mirror moves the sample locations to position 2. While the mirror is moving, the FPA samples from sub-image 1 are read-out. The scan mirror stabilizes at position 2 and sub-image 2 is collected. The time between sampling sub-image 1 and sub-image 2 is τ seconds. The mirror then moves the sample locations to position 3, and sub-image 3 is collected. The process is repeated for sub-image 4. If the scene is static, the effective sample spacing both horizontally and vertically is 0.5 mrad when all of the sub-images are combined. If the scene is static, the horizontal and vertical dither patterns are mathematically separable. That is, the horizontal and vertical increase in sampling can be treated separately.

Figure 5.7 illustrates diagonal dither. Diagonal dither improves image sampling both horizontally and vertically. However, as is shown below, neither the horizontal nor vertical sample rate is doubled. The diagonal dither cannot be treated as separable.

Horizontal or vertical dither doubles the sample rate in the respective axis. Horizontal dither is used as an example. Refer back to Chapter 3. An image is sampled by multiplying by a comb of impulse functions. The displayed image is then reconstructed by convolving the display pixel shape over the delta function samples. Remember that $p_{ix}(x)$ is the intensity distribution associated with a single display pixel, and $P_{ix}(\xi)$ is the Fourier transform. Remember also that $h(x)$ is the pre-sample blur, $s_{cn}(x)$ is the scene intensity distribution, and X is the sample spacing. For the present example, X is the sample spacing in one field or sub-image. The display is generated by summing two sample sets taken τ time apart. In a manner similar to Equation 3.2, the displayed image is represented by

$$i_{dsp}(x) = \{[h(x) * s_{cn}(x-d)] \sum_{n=-\infty}^{\infty} \delta(x-nX)\} * p_{ix}(x) \text{ samples taken at } t_0$$

$$+ \{[h(x) * s_{cn}(x-d)] \sum_{n=-\infty}^{\infty} \delta(x-nX-X/2)\} * p_{ix}(x) \text{ samples taken at } t_0 + \tau.$$

$$(5.1)$$

As long as the scene is static, $s_{cn}(x)$ is not a function of time. The samples can be described by a single sum.

$$\sum_{n=-\infty}^{\infty} \delta(x-nX) + \sum_{n=-\infty}^{\infty} \delta(x-nX-X/2) = \sum_{n=-\infty}^{\infty} \delta(x-nX/2). \qquad (5.2)$$

The result shown in Equation 5.3 is identical to Equation 3.2 but with the X sample spacing halved. The sample rate is doubled by horizontal or vertical interlace or dither.

$$i_{dsp}(x) = \{[h(x) * s_{cn}(x-d)] \sum_{n=-\infty}^{\infty} \delta(x-nX/2)\} * p_{ix}(x). \qquad (5.3)$$

The improved sample rate can be illustrated in the Fourier domain. Equations 3.4 through 3.7 give the sampled response for an image generated with a single field. Equation 5.4 shows the sampled response which results from adding two fields or sub-images. The expression in Equation 5.4 is based on a static scene and on a change in sample phase ϕ of 180 degrees or π radians between fields.

$$R_{sp}(\xi) = P_{ix}(\xi) \sum_{n=-\infty}^{\infty} H(\xi - n\nu) S_{cn}(\xi - n\nu) e^{-jn\phi} \quad (field\ 1)$$

$$+ \quad P_{ix}(\xi) \sum_{n=-\infty}^{\infty} H(\xi - n\nu) S_{cn}(\xi - n\nu) e^{-jn(\phi+\pi)} \quad (field\ 2). \tag{5.4}$$

For n odd, the two terms in Equation 5.4 are of equal amplitude but 180 degrees out of phase. For n even, the two terms are equal. Therefore,

$$R_{sp}(\xi) = 2 P_{ix}(\xi) \sum_{n=-\infty}^{\infty} H(\xi - n2\nu) S_{cn}(\xi - n2\nu) e^{-j2n\phi} \tag{5.5}$$

and the sample frequency effectively doubles.

Diagonal dither is illustrated in Figure 5.7. In order to describe diagonal dither, the sampling expression in Equation 3.2 is expressly shown as two dimensional in Equation 5.6. To simplify the expression, $f(x,y)$ is substituted for the convolution of $h(x,y)$ and $s_{cn}(x,y)$; that is, $f(x,y)$ is the pre-sample image. Separability of the pre-sample image function is still assumed, so that $f(x,y) = f_x(x)f_y(y)$.

$$i_{dsp}(x,y,t_0) = \{ [f_x(x) \sum_{n=-\infty}^{\infty} \delta(x - nX)] * p_{ixx}(x) \} \{ [f_y(y) \sum_{m=-\infty}^{\infty} \delta(y - mY)] * p_{ixy}(y) \}. \tag{5.6}$$

Equation 5.6 represents the set of samples taken during the first field of the diagonal dither. The second set of samples is represented by Equation 5.7. In that equation, the image is moved rather than defining different sample locations. In Equation 5.1, the second set of samples are taken at different locations in space relative to the first set of samples. In Equation 5.7, the image is moved relative to the sample set; the location of the sample set is not changed. The representations are equivalent.

$$i_{dsp}(x,y,t_0 + \tau) = \{ [f_x(x - X/2) \sum_{n=-\infty}^{\infty} \delta(x - nX)] * p_{ixx}(x) \}$$

$$\{ [f_x(y - Y/2) \sum_{m=-\infty}^{\infty} \delta(y - mY)] * p_{ixy}(y) \}. \tag{5.7}$$

Chapter 3 provides the details for finding the Fourier transforms of Equations 5.6 and 5.7. The sample phase is assumed to be zero for this example; this reduces equation complexity without affecting the conclusions.

$$I_{dsp}(\xi,\eta,t_0) = P_{ixx}(\xi) \sum_{n=-\infty}^{\infty} F_x(\xi - n\nu_x) P_{ixy}(\eta) \sum_{m=-\infty}^{\infty} F_y(\eta - m\nu_y) \qquad (5.8)$$

$$I_{dsp}(\xi,\eta,t_0 + \tau) = P_{ixx}(\xi) \sum_{n=-\infty}^{\infty} F_x(\xi - n\nu_x) e^{-j2\pi(\xi - n\nu_x)X/2}$$
$$P_{ixy}(\eta) \sum_{m=-\infty}^{\infty} F_y(\eta - m\nu_y) e^{-j2\pi(\eta - m\nu_y)Y/2} \qquad (5.9)$$

$$I_{dsp}(\xi,\eta) = P_{ixx}(\xi) \sum_{n=-\infty}^{\infty} F_x(\xi - n\nu_x) P_{ixy}(\eta) \sum_{m=-\infty}^{\infty} F_y(\eta - m\nu_y)$$
$$[1 + (-1)^n (-1)^m e^{-j\pi\xi X} e^{-j\pi\eta Y}]. \qquad (5.10)$$

In Equation 5.10, the $e^{-j2\pi n\nu_x X/2}$ factor reduces to $(-1)^n$ because $\nu_x = 1/X$.

The Fourier transform in Equation 5.10 is not separable. That is, the Fourier transform cannot be factored into a function of ξ and a function of η. It follows from Fourier transform theory that the space function is not separable either. That is, the pre-sample function $f(x,y)$ is separable, but after sampling with diagonal dither, the result is generally not separable.

The Fourier transform in Equation 5.10 is separable if either $f_x(x)$ or $f_y(y)$ is constant. For example, if the scene is a vertical bar pattern, the diagonal dither provides the same sampling performance as double sampling in the horizontal direction. If the scene is a horizontal bar pattern, then the vertical sampling rate is effectively doubled. However, for other than these bland or very regular scenes, the sampling is not effectively doubled on either axis.

If a diagonally dithered sensor is tested in the lab using horizontal and vertical bars or slits or edges, the conclusion might be that diagonal sampling doubles the effective sampling rate in both directions. This is not the case. A sensor can be characterized by tests using horizontal and vertical bars only if the sensor system MTF is separable. The image resulting from the diagonal dither process is not separable. A diagonal dither does not provide a doubled sample rate in both the horizontal and vertical directions. The authors believe that diagonal dither increases the "equivalent" sample rate by the square root of two in both the horizontal and vertical directions.

5.2 RESOLUTION AND SENSITIVITY

Dither improves sample rate for a static scene. But, dither cannot improve either the pre-sample MTF or the sensor transfer response.

Figure 5.8 shows the transfer response (dark line) and spurious response for an undersampled sensor. The figure abscissa is frequency normalized to the sample rate, and the ordinate gives amplitude. The sensor is undersampled because the spurious response overlaps the transfer response of the system. This sensor has in-band aliasing. In-band aliasing cannot be corrected at the display. In-band aliasing can only be removed by better sampling. As shown at the bottom of the figure, adding dither doubles the sample rate and eliminates the in-band aliasing.

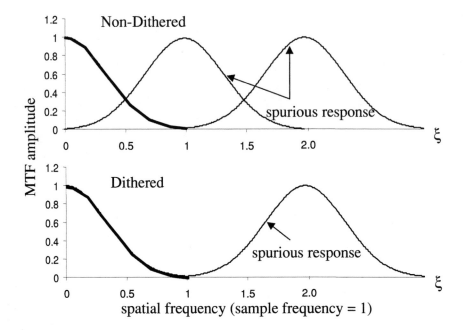

Figure 5.8 Top shows sampled response when dither is not used. The spurious response overlaps the transfer response (shown as a dark line). The in-band spurious response (spurious response below 0.5 on the frequency axis) cannot be removed by display processing. Bottom graph shows sampled spectrum when dither is used. Spurious response no longer overlaps the baseband; in-band aliasing is avoided.

The pre-sample MTF and resulting transfer response can be degraded if the dither mirror is not stationary during the time the detector integrates scene signal. Scene-to-sensor motion during the detector dwell time causes motion blur. MTF can also be reduced if there is a discrepancy between the sample position on the FPA and the corresponding pixel position on the display. However, given that the microscanner positions the focal plane correctly and stabilizes the image on the detector for the signal integration period, then the dithering action only increases the sampling rate.

For a well-sampled imaging system, no benefit is seen with dithering. But, for an undersampled imaging system, dithering provides a reduction or elimination of in-band aliasing.

Dither may or may not change the sensitivity of an imaging system. The detector FPA cannot be collecting signal during dither mirror motion. The motion blur would be excessive. However, some detectors cannot integrate signal for the whole 1/60th of a second available at the typical display rate.

For example, an InSb imager with an $F/3$ optical system has a typical integration time of 1 millisecond. The integration time is limited to the time it takes for the integration capacitor to fill up with photon-generated electrons. At the typical 60 Hertz display rate, the imager has 17 milliseconds to collect samples. The InSb sensor can capture multiple sub-images during each 1/60th of a second without loss of sensitivity.

One possible timing diagram for an InSb sensor with dither is shown in Figure 5.9. Standard video display format is assumed; there are 60 display fields per second with 2:1 vertical interlace resulting in a 30 Hertz frame rate. This example provides a 2:1 improvement in both horizontal and vertical sampling.

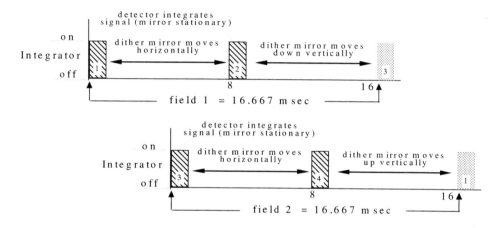

Figure 5.9 Dither timing diagram for InSb sensor. Diagram shows detector integrating signal for 1 millisecond at each dither location. Dither mirror moves sample locations during dead time between detector samples. The spatial scan pattern is shown in Figure 5.10. The spatial location of each sample is indicated by the number. In this example, samples from two dither locations are used to generate one field of displayed video. A frame of video consists of the two fields shown. A video frame contains samples from four dither locations.

Two possibilities for the spatial sampling pattern are shown in Figure 5.10. The detector integrates signal for about 1 millisecond at position 1 and time 0. During this period, the dither mirror is stationary. After the detector circuit stops integrating signal, the dither mirror moves horizontally to a second position and stabilizes. The second position changes the horizontal sample phase by 180 degrees; that is, the image is translated by one-half pixel horizontally. While the mirror is changing positions, the InSb array must output to digital memory all of the samples collected at position 1. The mirror stabilizes at position 2, and the detector collects samples at that position at time 8 milliseconds. These samples are subsequently read-out of the FPA. The two sub-images are combined in memory, and an image with improved horizontal resolution is displayed during the first display field.

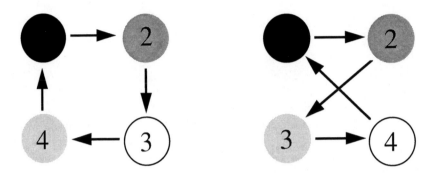

Figure 5.10 Dither patterns used to improve horizontal resolution and provide vertical interlace. The black, dark gray, light gray, and white dots represent sample locations. The numbers in the dots represent location sequence.

The image is then dithered by one-half pixel vertically and two sub-images collected for the next display field. Again, the second display field has improved horizontal resolution, because two sub-images are combined electronically before the display. Improved vertical resolution is provided by the vertical interlace.

For the dithering to be effective, the microscan mirror must change positions accurately and stabilize quickly. Further, the InSb array must be capable of outputting all of the FPA samples at a 120 Hertz rate. Given these capabilities, however, the extra samples provided by dither are achieved without loss in sensitivity.

In contrast, a PtSi system with the same optics integrates for 16 milliseconds. Even with a zero microscanner movement time, the detector integration time for a two-point field dither would be cut to 8 milliseconds. This factor of two reduction in detector integration time results in a square root of two reduction in signal to noise. Allowing realistic time for mirror motion, the sensitivity loss for PtSi would be substantial.

However, with today's technology, dither is most needed when using a low resolution InSb or HgCdTe FPA with up to 256 by 256 elements. These arrays have high quantum efficiencies and have limited photo-electron integration times. These qualities make dither attractive, because the improved sampling provided by dither can be achieved without significant loss of sensitivity.

5.3 EFFECT OF SCENE-TO-SENSOR MOTION

Dither can lead to motion artifacts like doubled or jerky images. To avoid motion artifacts, imagery should be collected and displayed with the same time sequence. That is, to completely avoid motion artifacts, imagery collected in one sensor field should not be displayed more than once. Imagery collected in multiple sensor fields at different times should not be combined into one display field. Dither is not yet common in fielded systems. But the problems associated with using different update rates for the sensor and display are well documented.

There can be significant, practical advantage to capturing imagery at a different rate than it is displayed. Movies at the local cinema work exactly this way. A movie is recorded by shooting 24 pictures a second; each picture is projected twice to avoid perceptible flicker. This technique saves a lot of film.

Projecting each picture twice results in motion artifacts. Cameramen are taught to pan the camera slowly, and slow shutter speeds are used to blur the image. Keeping the audience from noticing the motion artifacts is part of the art of film making. The next time you are at the theater, look closely; you will see a double or jerky image as the camera pans a scene.

The "standard" next generation thermal imager originally operated at a 30 Hertz frame rate and was not interlaced. Display flicker was avoided by displaying each image twice; the first field of a standard video display was new sensor imagery, and the second field was a replication of the first field.

Non-interlace operation at 30 Hertz was chosen for compatibility with digital image processing. Non-interlace operation provides a fully sampled "snapshot" for image processing regardless of scene motion. Thirty Hertz sensor operation was chosen rather than 60 Hertz because it provides better sensitivity for the processor, the mechanical scanner is easier to build and more efficient, and system throughput would be doubled. The doubling of throughput requires doubling the bandwidth of system components.

As with the movies, however, this display technique leads to motion artifacts. Unlike the movies, clear vision during rapid image motion can be critical in many applications. Two military examples where an operator must perform a visual task during scene-to-sensor motion include using a targeting sensor to rapidly search an area and using a pilotage sensor to fly a helicopter. During the execution of these tasks, the operator sees doubled, jerky, or blurred images, and these artifacts can be very pronounced. Normal eye and head movement make the motion artifacts particularly annoying in night helicopter pilotage systems which use head-tracked sensors and helmet-mounted displays.

The motion artifacts described in this section are quite real and can be quite annoying to system users. Based on experiments and strong feedback from users, all next generation imagers either operate at 60 Hertz or are equipped with a "30 or 60 Hertz" switch so that the user can select a mode without these artifacts. First generation thermal imagers built with 4:1 interlace and displayed at 2:1 were discarded after the bothersome artifacts disappointed the customers.

In order to discuss the expected magnitude of the motion artifact problem, consider the two dither implementations illustrated in Figures 5.9 and 5.10. Remember that a video field is 16.67 milliseconds long, and there are two video fields per video frame. Image samples taken 8 milliseconds apart are combined to form video field 1. Another set of image samples taken 8 milliseconds apart are combined to form field 2.

This dither implementation captures two images and combines them into a single picture. This is a double exposure. If scene motion occurs, the result is a blurred or double image. Two views of the moving object are presented by each display field.

Whether the blur or double image is bothersome or even noticeable depends on many factors. Those factors include motion rate, the field of view of the sensor, the transfer function of the sensor, the field of view of the display at the eye, display blur, and the nature of the task being performed. To calculate the visual offset angle V_{off} in degrees at the eye, let P_{rate} be the pixels per second motion on the display, P_{ang} represent the angle in degrees of one display pixel at the eye, and τ be the time between sub-images (8 milliseconds in the above example).

$$V_{off} = P_{rate}\, P_{ang}\, \tau. \tag{5.11}$$

Based on experience with a variety of military systems and tasks, limiting τ to 8 milliseconds or less results in imagery which is suitable for most purposes. However, the artifacts resulting from τ values between 16 and 33 milliseconds make imagery unsuitable for some military tasks.

It should be emphasized that none of the discussion in Section 5.3 applies to interlace. Interlaced sensors acquire and display image samples in a time synchronous manner. The artifacts described in this section arise from a disconnect between the rate at which imagery is acquired by the sensor and the rate at which it is displayed to the observer. The artifacts are not caused by sampling only part of the field of view in each field, as long as the sensor and display act together.

BIBLIOGRAPHY

Friedenberg, A., "Microscan in Infrared Staring Systems," Opt. Eng., Vol. 38, pp. 1745-1749, 1997.

Mikoshiba, A., G. Izumi, T. Nakamura, and K. Igarashi, "Appearance of False Pixels and Degradation of Picture Quality in Matrix Displays Having Extended Light-Emission Periods," SID Digest, Vol. XXIII, pp. 659-662, 1992.

Vollmerhausen, R. and T. Bui, "The Effect of Sensor Field Replication on Displayed Imagery," SID Digest, Vol. XXVI, pp. 667-670, 1995.

6

DYNAMIC SAMPLING, RESOLUTION ENHANCEMENT, AND SUPER RESOLUTION

This chapter contributed by:

Jonathon M. Schuler, Dean A. Scribner
Optical Sciences Division
U.S. Naval Research Laboratory
Washington, DC 20375

6.1 INTRODUCTION

As developed in Chapter 3, FPA camera design trades blur with aliasing, both of which degrade the imager performance. Such analysis assumes a fixed spatial sampling rate at the camera focal plane, determined by the detector pitch of the FPA. If an FPA camera system can *dynamically sample* the optical image, then the FPA sampling rate no longer limits the resolution of the digitally sampled imagery.

There is considerable historical experience with dynamically sampled camera systems, particularly with first generation FLIRs. Simply scanning a 1-D column of detectors, or even a single detector element, can generate 2-D imagery with obviously higher spatial resolution than that of the single column or element. Such processing critically hinges on accurate knowledge of the scanning motion, which is often a precisely controlled function of the servo voltage that drives a scanning mirror assembly. Fusing such position information with detector intensity information generates the higher resolution imagery.

Two-dimensional micro-dither scanning can likewise increase the spatial resolution of an FPA camera. However such 2-D micro-dither scanning involves mechanical complexities beyond first generation scanning FLIRs. Such processing requires longer framing times, introduces jitter distortions, and increases the sensor weight and complexity: Precisely the problems that motivated the engineering of FPA cameras in lieu of scanning sensors!

As an alternative to controlled micro-dither scanning, the optical flow of an image sequence can be computed to tag a spatial coordinate with every pixel of the video sequence. Intensity and coordinate information can then be combined to create an image with higher sampling density than that of the FPA. Such uncontrolled micro-dither scanning retains the speed and simplicity of an FPA camera while significantly improving image resolution through oversampling. These benefits come by off-loading the scanning process from physical hardware to digital electronics.

Such optical-flow based micro-scanning forces a re-examination of acceptable design trades between optical blur and aliasing. Sharper optics can now be used, provided the optical flow can be computed despite aliasing. Additional considerations can trade faster FPA frame rate for image latency, depending on the desired sampling density and noise performance of the FPA.

6.2 SAMPLING LIMITATIONS OF THE FOCAL PLANE ARRAY TOPOLOGY

6.2.1 Review of discrete image sampling

Section 2.4 summarizes discrete sampling of an optical image by a spatially integrating photo-detector array. We reconstruct that analysis, beginning with a scene function, $\Psi(x,y,t)$, which describes the radiant intensity of the world (object plane) relative to camera coordinates. Given the spectral response of a camera system, this function has units of spectrally integrated photons per unit time per unit area. Also note that this function has unbounded spatial frequency content and limitless detail. Any ideal lens geometrically projects the scene function onto the focal plane to create scaled replica with the same physical units and spatial frequency detail.

$$s_{geometric}(x,y,t) \propto \Psi\left(\frac{x}{m_x}, \frac{y}{m_y}, t\right) \quad m_x, m_y = \text{geometric scaling factors.} \quad (6.1)$$

All cameras invariably employ a lens of limited spatial fidelity and project an optical image onto an array of sampling detectors positioned at the focal plane. The resulting *pseudo-image* signal is degraded due to both lens blur and spatial integration of the finite sized photo-detector, characterized by the combined linear spatial convolution of the signal with these effects.

$$s_{pseudo}(x,y,t) = h_{pixel}(x,y) ** h_{psf}(x,y) ** s_{geometric}(x,y,t). \quad (6.2)$$

The spatial extent of an ideal photo-detector pixel with uniform response across dimensions $[a_x, a_y]$ serves as a "box car" integrator of the geometric image with the pixel impulse response:

$$h_{pixel}(x,y) = rect\left(\frac{x}{a_x}\right) rect\left(\frac{y}{a_y}\right). \quad (6.3)$$

The lens point spread function may be ideally modeled as the diffraction limited Airy disk. In practice, the lens point spread function is often modeled as a circularly symmetric Gaussian blur.

Integrating and reading out the photo-detector array with detector pitches $\left[b_x, b_y \right]$ at a clock rate t_{clock} digitizes the pseudo-image, creating a discrete representation.

$$s_{digital}\left[n_x, n_y, n_t \right] = s_{pseudo}\left(n_x b_x, n_y b_y, n_t t_{clock} \right). \tag{6.4}$$

This resulting discrete data structure is fundamentally different from the continuous pseudo-image. Whereas the Continuous Space Fourier Transform (CSFT) for a two-dimensional aperiodic signal is an integral over all space,

$$S\left(\xi, \eta \right) = \int_{-\infty}^{\infty} \int_{-\infty}^{\infty} s\left(x, y \right) \; e^{-j2\pi\xi x} \; e^{-j2\pi\eta y} dx \; dy. \tag{6.5}$$

the Discrete Space Fourier Transform of a sampled two-dimensional aperiodic signal is a summation over a countable set of sample positions.

$$S\left(\xi, \eta \right) = \sum_{-\infty}^{\infty} \sum_{-\infty}^{\infty} s[m, n] e^{-j\xi n} e^{-j\eta n}. \tag{6.6}$$

These differences are characterized by their relationship to one another, where the DSFT of the digital image is a periodic extension of the CSFT of the pseudo-image.

$$S_{digital}\left(\xi, \eta, n_t \right) = \frac{1}{b_x} \frac{1}{b_y} \sum_k \sum_l S_{pseudo}\left(\frac{\xi - k}{b_x}, \frac{\eta - l}{b_y}, n_t t_{clock} \right) \tag{6.7}$$

Note that discrete frequency is related to continuous frequency by

$$\eta = \frac{F_y}{F_{sample}} = b_y F_y.$$

6.2.2 The fundamental limitation of the FPA sampling

Consider a one-dimensional FPA camera, consisting of a line of detectors illuminated by a geometric optic with arbitrarily narrow blur width. Because of the finite detector of size a, the resulting imagery is distorted with an MTF determined by the Continuous Space Fourier Transform of this spatial "box car" integrator, given by $a\left(\frac{\sin(aF)}{aF} \right)$ and plotted in Figure 6.1 for $a = 1$.

By itself, such detector "box car" blur can be fully recovered for all but a countable number of spatial harmonics given a noiseless detector and a suitably chosen restoration filter.

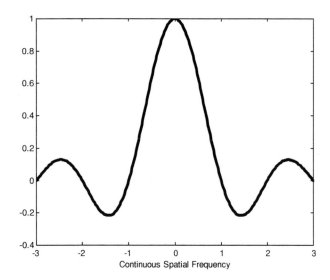

Figure 6.1 MTF of an ideal 1-D pixel.

By sampling the output of each photo-detector at every lattice site separated by a distance b, we generate a discrete data structure whose Discrete Space Fourier Transform is given by the infinite sum

$$S_{digital}(\xi) = \frac{a}{b} \sum_{k=-\infty}^{\infty} \frac{\sin\left(aF - \frac{k}{b}\right)}{aF - \frac{k}{b}}.$$ (6.8)

Figure 6.2 plots this sum for $a_1 = 1$ and $b_1 = 1$, corresponding to a 100% fill factor detector array. This plot underscores the profound aliasing endemic with common FPA topologies, where all but the lowest of spatial frequencies suffer from alias corruption due to an inadequate spatial sampling rate.

This aliasing can be reduced if the sampling rate is artificially increased through some form of synthetic sampling, such as micro dithering or scanning. Synthetically increasing this sampling rate by a dither factor D generates a Discrete Spatial Frequency Response given by

$$S_{dithered}(\xi) = \frac{a}{Db} \sum_{k} \frac{\sin\left(\dfrac{aF - \dfrac{k}{b}}{D}\right)}{\dfrac{aF - \dfrac{k}{b}}{D}}.$$ (6.9)

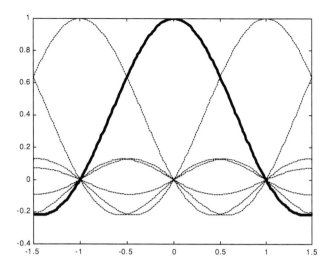

Figure 6.2 MTF of a 1-D pixel array.

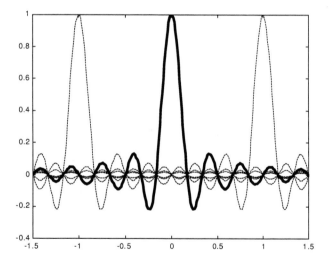

Figure 6.3 MTF of a dithered 1-D pixel array.

Figure 6.3 plots the Discrete Spatial Frequency Response for a FPA dithered by a factor $D = 6$. Note that although the $\dfrac{\sin(x)}{x}$ attenuation of the dithered FPA pixel is enhanced on the Discrete Spatial Frequency domain $\left[-\dfrac{\pi}{2}, \dfrac{\pi}{2}\right]$, the aliasing is significantly reduced.

6.3 DYNAMIC SAMPLING

FPA based camera systems must accommodate the intrinsically poor sampling rate of FPA topology. Good camera engineering always tolerates some aliasing, and any pseudo-image will invariably contain spatial frequencies higher than the FPA can properly sample.

Synthetically increasing the sampling rate of FPA cameras through dithering can reduce that aliasing. A composite image constructed from a super-sampled sequence can subsequently be restored to reveal details unachievable by any single frame of video.

In its simplest form, dynamic sampling can be achieved by a mechanically actuated, uniformly spaced micro-dither scan. Interlacing the constituent images creates a super-sampled image with reduced aliasing and higher resolution. Scanner stability requirements limit this procedure to strictly controlled environments and have achieved up to four-fold increases in the spatial sampling rate.

In practice, frames of digital imagery acquired from a moving platform undergo geometric perspective transformations, resulting in image differences that cannot be measured by a single shift, nor interlaced to generate a higher sampling density image.

Figure 6.4 demonstrates that the optical flow for two frames of an FPA camera, separated by $1/25^{th}$ second in time, is not a uniform shift but a spatially dependent flow field. It is such a non-uniform flow that plagues all scanning imaging systems whose reconstruction algorithm depends on a uniform shift assumption.

6.4 AMBIENT OPTICAL FLOW AS A NOVEL SAMPLING MECHANISM

A more flexible approach to controlled micro-dither scanning accepts the non-uniform optical flow of a scan sequence. By precisely computing the motion and assigning every pixel a time-varying coordinate, the scan sequence can be re-sorted into a single image of higher sampling density. Because the motion is not controlled, the higher sampling density is true only in a statistical sense, and still suffers from errors due to non-uniform sampling. Although interpolation can address this problem, such distortion is empirically small compared to the overall distortions of electronic noise and signal digitization

6.4.1 Shift estimation

Generic optical flow computation is founded on robust estimation of a single shift between images. Figure 6.5 demonstrates two uniformly shifted images generated by a 256×256 window of the *Lena* image that was horizontally shifted by 6 pixels.

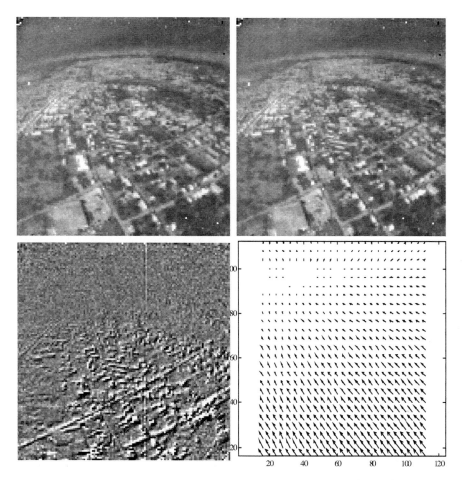

Figure 6.4 Two frames of aerial imagery, separated $1/25^{th}$ second, from an undersampled sensor (top). Difference image between these two images (bottom left). Optical flow of this image sequence (bottom right). Note the spatially varying optical flow, with the greatest flow occurring at points closest to the sensor.

Figure 6.5 256 by 256 windows of an image displaced by 6 horizontal pixels (left, center). Difference image (right).

One solution to this displacement estimation problem is to apply *Gradient Estimation*, which derives a sub-pixel shift estimate between two images through a first- order Taylor expansion of the difference between both images:

$$\hat{S} = \frac{1}{4}\frac{\sum\left(y_{n+1} - x_{n+1} + y_n - x_n\right)\left(y_{n+1} - y_n + x_{n+1} - x_n\right)}{\sum\left(x_{n+1} - x_n\right)^2}. \qquad (6.10)$$

The Taylor expansion used in *Gradient Estimation* is valid in the limit of small shift displacements. Larger displacements degrade the performance of this technique.

More commonly, displacement is inferred from the spatial *Correlation* between the two shifted images. The spatial correlation for 2-D discrete images is defined by the convolution between those two images:

$$\Phi[m,n] = \sum_{\mu=-\infty}^{\mu=\infty} \sum_{\mu=-\infty}^{\mu=\infty} I_1[m+\mu, n+\nu] I_2[m,n]. \qquad (6.11)$$

Figure 6.6 demonstrates that the resulting $\Phi[m,n]$ for two slightly displaced images is generally a concave function whose single maximum occurs at the actual shift displacement.

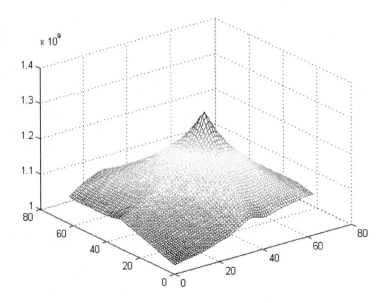

Figure 6.6 Correlation plot for two displaced images.

Because convolution is a Linear Space Invariant operation, correlation can be expressed as the product of two DSFTs in the discrete spatial frequency domain.

$$\Phi(\xi,\eta) = I_1(\xi,\eta)\ I_2(\xi,\eta), \quad \text{where} \quad S(\xi,\eta) = \sum_{-\infty}^{\infty}\sum_{-\infty}^{\infty} s[m,n]e^{-i\xi m}e^{-i\eta n}. \qquad (6.12)$$

This technique can quickly exploit the fast Fourier transform to significantly reduce computational burdens. Because such computational correlation plots are sampled at the same density as the images, a simple maximum threshold to determine the correlation peak is only accurate to 1 pixel. The 2-D curve fitting can generate a parameterized function that yields a sub-pixel estimate of the displacement.

Phase correlation analyzes the Fourier phase of two images. This technique can be applied to high SNR imagery with improved performance over correlation. This method has the added benefit of insensitivity to overall brightness changes between images, which can heavily degrade the performance of other image displacement estimation methods.

The phase of an image is defined as the Fourier transform of the image normalized to unity magnitude and is demonstrated in Figure 6.7.

$$S_{phase}(\xi,\eta) = \frac{S(\xi,\eta)}{|S(\xi,\eta)|}, \quad \text{where} \quad S(\xi,\eta) = \sum_{-\infty}^{\infty}\sum_{-\infty}^{\infty} s[m,n]e^{-i\xi m}e^{-i\eta n}. \tag{6.13}$$

Figure 6.7 Image (left) and its reconstructed Fourier phase (right).

Figure 6.8 demonstrates how the phase correlation has a more distinct surface peak for the same displaced image pair.

Maximum Likelihood methods have been applied with limited success to the displacement estimation process. Overall, ML methods specify the power spectra for the underlying image and additive noise in the image acquisition process. Invariably, such models apply a Poisson process to the image pixels subject to additive white Gaussian noise from the acquisition process. The logarithm of the joint Probability Density Function between two such uniformly displaced images becomes a quadratic function ripe for minimization analysis. Not surprisingly, these methods work quite well for numerical simulations of auto-regressive generated textures. In practice, their application on real imagery has limited published success.

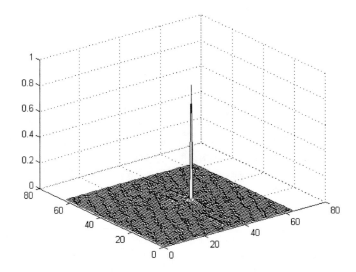

Figure 6.8 Phase correlation for the displaced image pair.

6.4.2 Generalized motion estimation

The general motion estimation problem involves images that differ not by a simple translation, but by a more complex *optical flow*. There is a large body of robotic vision literature that addresses the case of a stationary camera observing moving objects, particularly in manufacturing and intrusion detection. Our development is applied to the complementary situation of a moving camera observing a stationary scene. Everyday experiences with walking, driving, or flying reveal an intuitive, distance dependent scene shift that plays a significant role in our psychophysical balance and orientation. Simple shift estimation invariably proves to be insufficient at characterizing the global, non-uniform optical flow between two images taken from such moving platforms with wide field-of-view optics.

In the limit of smaller window sizes, the optical flow better approximates that of a single, uniform shift suitable for the estimation techniques previously described. This suggests a simple approach to computing the global optical flow: By repeatedly applying a uniform displacement estimator to some small local window that slides across the entire image, a crude estimate of the global optical flow can be mapped, as shown in Figure 6.9

Figure 6.10 demonstrates how this array of noisy shift estimates can be least squares fit to a parametric motion model to generate a detailed optical flow estimate with considerable immunity to the error of any individual uniform-shift estimate.

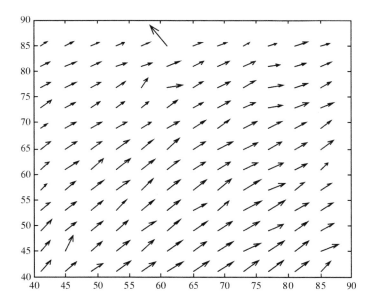

Figure 6.9 Crude map of the optical flow between two displaced images, generated by repeated application of a uniform shift estimator applied to a smaller aperture than the full image.

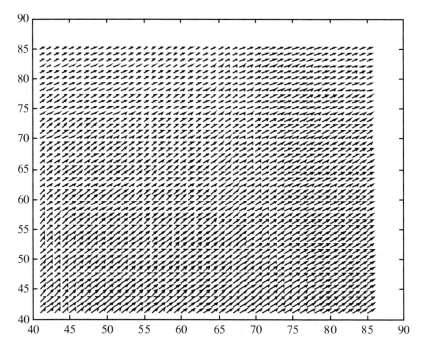

Figure 6.10 Detailed optical flow estimate generated by parametrically modeling the crude optical flow of Figure 6.9 to a simple linear perspective transformation.

6.5 IMAGE RESTORATION

Once the optical flow has been computed for a time window of video, the 3-D cube of pixel intensities needs to be re-sorted into a 2-D array of denser sampling points. At first order, such an array can be assembled on the criteria of which video pixel is spatially closest to a desired, uniformly spaced 2-D lattice. By itself, such an assembled image suffers from non-uniform sampling errors, which can be significant when compared to very low noise camera data. One path for coping is to interpolate such an array to the true uniform grid given the estimated non-uniform positions of the 3-D video sequence.

Nonetheless, the resulting array still suffers from heavy distortions as outlined in Section 6.1. A simple remedy is to apply a high-pass filter to compensate for known blur distortions. Figure 6.11 illustrates a single frame of video, a super-sampled composite derived from 16 frames of a sequence and the result of a simple model Wiener restoration filter.

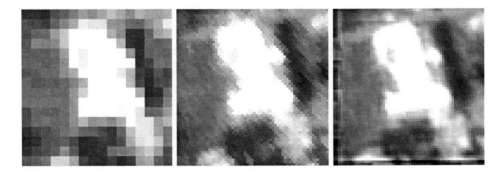

Figure 6.11 Original image (left). Super sampled composite (middle). Simple Wiener restoration (right).

The Wiener filter that restores a distorted *Pseudo-Image* to its original *Geometric Image* subject to known distortions of pixel and optical blur in the presence of additive, uncorrelated noise is given as:

$$G(\xi,\eta) = \frac{H^*(\xi,\eta)\ S_{Geo-Geo}(\xi,\eta)}{\left|H(\xi,\eta)\right|^2 S_{Geo-Geo}(\xi,\eta)\ +\ S_{noise-noise}(\xi,\eta)}. \tag{6.14}$$

For this example, $S_{Geo-Geo}(\xi,\eta)$ is the Power Spectral Density (PSD) of the *Geometric Image* and $S_{noise-noise}(\xi,\eta)$ is the PSD of the noise distortion. For this example, both were assumed to be spectrally flat, indexed to a crude Signal-To-Noise Parameter to yield a simplified restoration filter:

$$G(\xi,\eta) = \frac{H^*(\xi,\eta)\ SNR}{|H(\xi,\eta)|^2\ SNR\ +\ 1}. \tag{6.15}$$

The distortion term $H(\xi,\eta)$ represents the known distortions of pixels and optics. This was empirically determined by taking the Fourier transform of the square pixel distortion at the higher sample rate, modulated by a Gaussian envelope that approximates the optic PSF. Figure 6.12 plots the magnitude response of such a Wiener filter subject to a hypothetical 6-fold sampling increase under a 10-to-1 SNR.

Final choice of PSF blur and system SNR was left to a two-parameter search by hand to determine the parameter combination yielding the "best" image based on visual inspection.

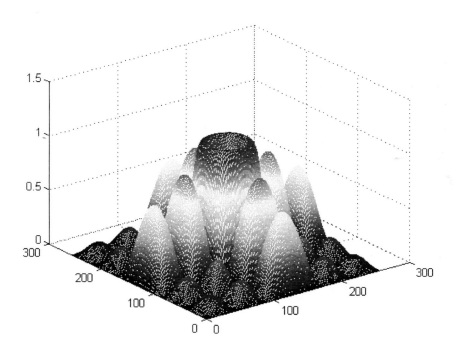

Figure 6.12 Spectral response of a Wiener restoration filter for a six-fold dithered image with a 10-1 SNR.

6.6 CONCLUSION

Because of the low spatial sampling rate of lattice-type FPA detectors in modern image sensors, the resulting sampled imagery suffers from alias distortions. Aliasing can be alleviated by increasing the sampling rate through some form of dithering or scanning and historically has worked well in imaging systems with few detectors. Although it is possible to micro-dither a 2-D FPA array to increase its spatial sampling rate, it comes at a high cost of mechanical complexity and dwell time. Because there is enough data within the alias-distorted 2-D imagery to apply motion estimation, one can *Dynamically Sample* a 2-D image from a 3-D video cube taken from short dwell image sequence subject to parametrically modeled platform motion.

Several points always need to be stressed with this technique:
1) This processing is fundamentally an *anti-aliasing* technique to improve image resolution. In a hypothetical case of a pseudo-image containing no alias distortion, this technique cannot improve system resolution.
2) This technique processes a time-window of video and is thus subject to a physically intrinsic latency.
3) This technique is fundamentally limited by sensor noise, which loosely bounds the upper limit of performance: Namely, one can continually super-sample and achieve improvement until the residual alias distortion is on the order of the sensor noise. This occurs when dithering to a density at roughly an SNR multiple of the FPA lattice density.

BIBLIOGRAPHY

Cain, S., E. Armstrong, and B. Yasuda "Joint Estimation of Image, Shifts, and NonUniformities from IR Images" Proceedings on the 1997 Meeting of the IRIS Specialty Group on Passive Sensors Vol. 1, 1997.

Horn, B.K.P. and B. G. Schunk, "Determining optical flow", *Artif. Intell.,* Vol. 17, pp. 185-204, 1981.

Jain, A. K., "Fundamentals of Digital Image Processing," Prentice Hall, 1989

Oppenheim, A. V. and A. S. Willsky, *Signals & Systems*, Prentice Hall, 1996.

Proakis, J. G. and D. G. Manolakis, *Digital Signal Processing*, Macmillan Publishing Company (1992).

Schaum, A. and M. McHugh, "Analytic Methods of Image Registration: Displacement Estimation and Resampling," NRL Report 9298 U.S. Naval Research Laboratory, Washington, DC (1992).

7

THE SAMPLING THEOREM

The Sampling Theorem is cited often in engineering circles, and a description of the theorem is a necessary part of a book on sampling. However, the Sampling Theorem represents an ideal limit. The Sampling Theorem substitutes ideal pre- and post-filters for the sensor and display MTF, respectively. As a result, the real system behavior is not characterized. The Sampling Theorem does not provide useful guidance for the design of EO imagers.

In this chapter, the Sampling Theorem is described and an example given of a near-ideal reconstruction of a sampled waveform. Also, some of the common misconceptions about the dictates of the Sampling Theorem will be discussed. Our primary purpose in describing the Sampling Theorem, however, is to demonstrate its limited value in evaluating real systems.

7.1 THEORY

The Sampling Theorem states that, for a signal $f(x)$ for which the Fourier transform has no components at or above frequency $f_{samp}/2$, the function can be entirely reconstructed by the series:

$$f(x) = \sum_{n=-\infty}^{\infty} f(n/f_{samp}) \frac{\sin(\pi x f_{samp} - n\pi)}{(\pi x f_{samp} - n\pi)}. \tag{7.1}$$

The function $f(x)$ is sampled with sample frequency f_{samp}. As discussed in Sections 1.5 and 3.1, the Fourier transform $F(\omega)$ of $f(x)$ is replicated at multiples of the sample frequency as shown in Figure 7.1. If the replicas of $F(\omega)$ do not overlap the baseband, meaning that $F(\omega)$ is band-limited to half the sample frequency, then $F(\omega)$ can be exactly reconstructed by using an ideal filter. This is also shown in Figure 7.1.

An ideal filter is a rect function, with MTF of one (1.0) out to half the sample frequency and zero beyond. The Fourier transform of a rect function is a sinc wave. Convolving the sampled data with a sinc wave in the spatial domain provides an ideal reconstruction filter in the frequency domain. Equation 7.1 represents the convolution in space. Each sample at location n/f_{samp} is convolved with the function $\sin(\pi x f_{samp})/(\pi x f_{samp})$. Since the samples are delta functions at the sample locations, Equation 7.1 represents the convolution.

The Sampling Theorem reconstruction is illustrated in Figure 7.2. Two samples are indicated by asterisks in Figure 7.2(a). For each sample, a sinc wave is generated with peak amplitude equal to the sample value. The period of each sinc wave is such that it goes through zero amplitude at every other sample location. The sum of all the sinc waves generated for all sample values is the reconstructed signal. The heavy, solid curve in Figure 7.2(b) shows the sum of the sinc waves for the two samples in Figure 7.2(a).

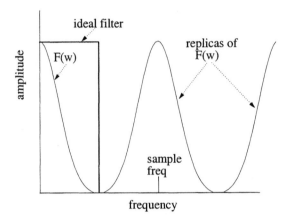

Figure 7.1 If the replicas of $F(w)$ do not overlap, then an ideal filter which cuts off at half the sample frequency will exactly recover the original function.

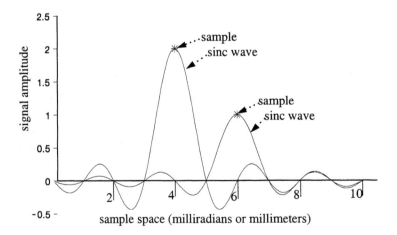

Figure 7.2(a) Example showing sinc wave reconstruction required by Sampling Theorem. In this example, the sample spacing is 1.0. Two samples are shown by asterisks at locations (4,2) and (6,1). Note that the sample at position 5,0 is not illustrated. For each sample, a sinc wave is generated with the peak equal to the sample value and period such that the sinc wave goes through zero amplitude at all other sample points.

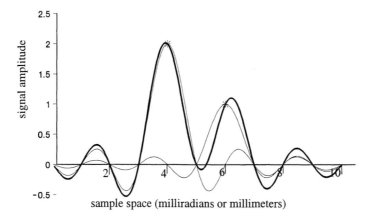

Figure 7.2(b)   To generate the reconstructed waveform, all sinc waves are added together. The sum of the two sinc waves shown in Figure 7.2(a) is shown here as the solid, dark line. This example only used two samples. In the general case, sinc waves are generated for all samples, and the sum of all sinc waves is the reconstructed waveform.

A band-limited function can be uniquely determined from its values at a sequence of equidistant points, $1/f_{samp}$ apart. The series in Equation 7.1 is used to reconstruct the function. Each term in the series is a sample function, also referred to as a sinc function or sinc wave. For each term in the series, the sinc wave amplitude is equal to the sample value, and the period is such that the sinc wave crosses zero at all other sample points. The function $f(x)$ is sampled over all space, and each sinc wave extends in both directions over all space.

7.2 EXAMPLE

If a sine wave is infinitely extended, then the Fourier transform is a delta function at the sine wave frequency and just over two samples per cycle is adequate to reconstruct the sampled waveform. The Sampling Theorem does not suggest, however, that a single cycle of a sine wave can be reconstructed by taking two samples. The Fourier transform of a single cycle of sine wave is shown in Figure 7.3; the sine wave has a period of one unit (milliradians or millimeters). Even using the first zero as the "band-limit," the sample rate would be 4.0 per cycle.

If the sample rate is just over two samples per cycle, an extended portion of the sine wave function must be sampled and reconstructed in order to accurately replicate any one cycle. The following illustrates this concept.

Figure 7.4 shows ten cycles of a sine wave; Figure 7.5 is the Fourier transform of those ten cycles. Taking the first zero in Figure 7.5 as an approximation to the "band-limit," the function is sampled 2.2 times per cycle. The asterisks in Figure 7.4 show the sample points.

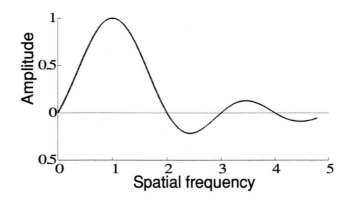

Figure 7.3 The Fourier transform of a single cycle of a sine wave with period of one. The Fourier transform of a sine wave is a single frequency only if the sine wave is infinitely extended.

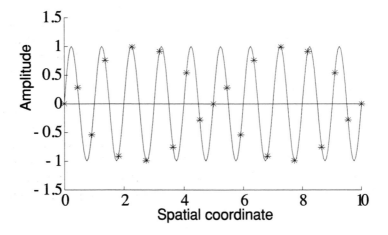

Figure 7.4 Ten cycles of a sine wave; the function is sampled 2.2 times per cycle at the asterisks.

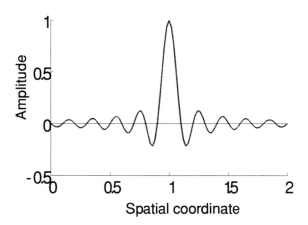

Figure 7.5 Fourier transform of ten sine wave periods shown in Figure 7.4.

Figure 7.6 shows the result of sampling and reconstructing the sixth period near the middle. Figure 7.7 shows the result of generating sinc waves for all 22 samples and adding them together. The sixth cycle is mainly reconstructed by contributions from neighboring cycles of the sine wave.

The sixth cycle is poorly sampled due to the sample phase. It reproduces well in the final result, because it is surrounded by other sampled periods of the sine wave. The edge cycles of the original ten sine wave periods are also poorly sampled. The edge cycles do not reconstruct to the full amplitude, because they have neighbors on only one side.

The Sampling Theorem states that a sine wave can be accurately reconstructed by taking just over two samples per cycle for an extended number of cycles. Each cycle of the sine wave is reconstructed by combining the sinc waves from all of the samples. Even if a large number of periods are sampled at just over two samples per cycle, the edges of the function will not be adequately reconstructed, because half the contributions from neighboring cycles are missing.

7.3 DISCUSSION

The Sampling Theorem states that, given a sufficient sample rate, a local region of a bandlimited function can be reconstructed from both local and remote samples of the function. The Sampling Theorem does not suggest that two or three samples will reconstruct a single cycle of a sine wave. Nor does the Sampling Theorem support the assertion that just over two samples per cycle of a three- or four-bar pattern are sufficient to reconstruct the pattern.

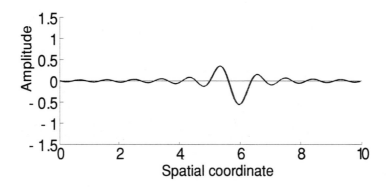

Figure 7.6 The sixth cycle is not properly reconstructed by using only the samples from that period.

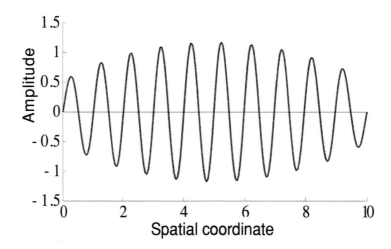

Figure 7.7 Reconstruction of Figure 7.4 using all 22 samples. Note that the sixth cycle is now properly reconstructed.

It is sometimes postulated that a single display pixel per sensor sample will provide the best image reconstruction possible with the sampled data. The shape of the display pixel is presumed to be arbitrary. This postulate is not consistent with the theory or the examples presented in this book. Looking at Equations 3.4 and 3.7 for real systems, the MTF of the display pixel filters both the transfer response and spurious content of the image. The shape of a display pixel is not arbitrary. Further, the discussion in Chapter 4 illustrates that multiple display pixels per sensor sample can often reduce the spurious content in an image while enhancing the transfer response.

While it is certainly true that a single display pixel might have the correct shape and size to produce a good looking image, nothing in sampling theory suggests that an optimum display is achieved by using one, arbitrarily shaped, display pixel per sensor sample.

Another assumption often made when modeling sampled imagers is that frequency content at up to half the sample rate is accurately imaged by the system. This assumption is incorrect if the imager has significant MTF response beyond half the sample rate. The Sampling Theorem states that a signal should be sampled at a rate more than twice the highest frequency present. There should be no frequency content at half the sample rate. The Sampling Theorem does not suggest that a sampled signal will be reconstructed accurately to half the sample rate; the latter assumption ignores any aliasing that might be present.

The Sampling Theorem assumes that the pre-sample image is ideally band-limited and that an ideal filter is used for image reconstruction at the display. However, for practical reasons, ideal filters are not implemented. As a result of the ideal filter assumption, however, the actual characteristics of the sensor and display are not quantified. The Sampling Theorem does not provide a basis for evaluating real systems since it is the compromises to the rules of the Sampling Theorem that are the essence of practical system design.

BIBLIOGRAPHY

Bracewell, R. N., *The Fourier Transform and Its Applications*, McGraw-Hill, New York, NY, 1986.

Gaskill, J., Linear Systems, *Fourier Transforms and Optics*, Wiley, New York, NY, 1978.

Goodman, J. W., *Introduction to Fourier Optics,* McGraw-Hill, San Francisco, CA, 1968.

Holst, G. C., *Sampling, Aliasing, and Data Fidelity,* SPIE Optical Engineering Press, Bellingham, WA, 1998.

Wozencraft, J. M. and I. M. Jacobs, *Principles of Communication Engineering*, Wiley, New York, NY, 1965.

8

LABORATORY MEASUREMENTS OF SAMPLED INFRARED IMAGING SYSTEM PERFORMANCE

An infrared imager (often referred to as a FLIR, from the term forward looking infrared) can be characterized in terms of sensitivity, resolution and human performance. Sensitivity, resolution and human performance have been classically described by the following measurable parameters: noise equivalent temperature difference (NETD), modulation transfer function (MTF) and minimum resolvable temperature difference (MRTD or MRT). These are laboratory measurable quantities that can be used to verify the performance of an infrared system. These laboratory measurements are used to evaluate expected design performance and to periodically test an imager during its life cycle. These quantities are predictable in sensor design through the use of analytical models. Both model estimates and laboratory measurements can be used in a target acquisition model to determine the field performance (probability of detection, recognition or identification) of the imager.

Sensitivity, resolution, and human performance are influenced by sampling artifacts that must be characterized. First, sensitivity is no longer sufficiently described by a single-valued NETD. The 3-D noise methodology, inhomogeneity equivalent temperature difference (IETD), and correctability are noise figures that have been developed over the past decade to more adequately describe both temporal and fixed pattern noise associated with focal plane arrays. Undersampled imaging systems are not shift-invariant. The shift-invariance condition, in particular, is compromised by under-sampling so that sensor performance becomes a function of phase (relative position between the image and the detector array). Resolution depends on the target-to-imager phase, so the MTF measurement may reveal sampling artifacts that give large MTF variations with target to sensor position. Finally, the human-performance parameter is perhaps most affected by undersampling. MRT can be strongly dependent on phase, where dramatic differences in measured MRT are attributed to different phase shifts. MRT is normally measured at optimum phase, yet the authors don't feel that static MRT measured with either optimum or unknown phase relationships correlate well with field performance. In the same way, it is not clear how to write field acquisition calculations based on MRT values measured past the half-sample (Nyquist) rate. A dynamic MRT method has been developed and measured which uses motion to provide enhanced sampling. It has been suggested that "DMRT" can provide part of the near-term solution to human performance estimates.

We begin with a description of the classical infrared performance parameters: NETD, MTF, and MRT. These measurements are still useful for analog scanning and other well-sampled imagers. The modifications and new measurements that are necessary to more fully characterize undersampled imaging systems are then described: The 3-D noise methodology, IETD, correctability, scanning slit/tilted edge MTF, and dynamic MRT. The issues associated with the testing of undersampled imaging systems are discussed and their application to target acquisition prediction is presented. Future trends for sampled imaging system measurements are also briefly discussed.

8.1 CLASSICAL INFRARED IMAGER PERFORMANCE MEASUREMENTS

8.1.1 Sensitivity

The classical infrared performance measure that describes the sensitivity of a sensor is called the Noise Equivalent Temperature Difference (NETD). It is defined as the blackbody temperature difference in a standard test pattern which produces a peak signal to rms-noise ratio of one at the output of a reference electronics filter. The measurement configuration is shown in Figure 8.1. A square target is placed at the focal plane of a collimator and is "back-lit" by a blackbody source. The image of the target is projected into the FLIR as shown. In the older, first generation FLIRs, the target could be in the right half of the field-of-view and the noise could be taken on the left half since the detectors scanned over the whole field-of-view. In today's staring arrays, the target has to be placed in the detector region of the noise measurement and then taken away. The external reference filter was applied to systems with analog detectors. NETD is now commonly reported without applying any external filter. In fact, NETD is extremely confusing because of the bandwidth that is used to describe NETD. In the well-known FLIR92 performance model, the NETD uses a bandwidth described by $4/\pi\tau_d$ where τ_d describes the response of the reference filter. In other NETD calculations, the noise filter bandwidth is set to $1/2\tau_d$, where τ_d is the integration time or the dwell time of the detector. NETD is sometimes specified where τ_d is the maximum possible detector integration time corresponding to the frame rate and not the actual integration time. (That is, if a staring sensor operates at 60 Hertz, the then possible dwell time is 16.667 milliseconds. This possible dwell time might be used even if the actual dwell or integration time is only 1 to 5 milliseconds.) It is important to describe the noise bandwidth definition with any NETD that is reported. In this chapter, we describe system noise by the spatio-temporal noise parameter, σ_{tvh}, as discussed in Section 8.2.

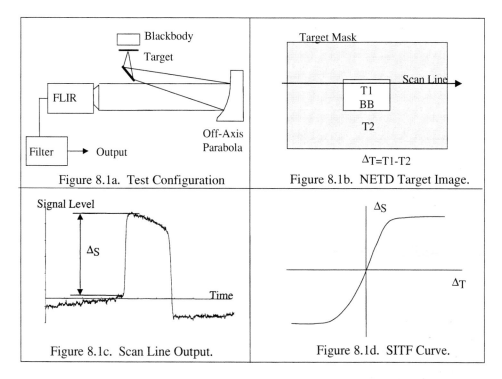

Figure 8.1a. Test Configuration

Figure 8.1b. NETD Target Image.

Figure 8.1c. Scan Line Output.

Figure 8.1d. SITF Curve.

Figure 8.1 Noise Equivalent Temperature Difference Measurement.

The NETD target image is shown in Figure 8.1(b). The target width and height should be no smaller than 10 times the detector angular subtense (of the FLIR under test) and no larger than 10% of the FLIR field-of-view. The target is defined by a circular or rectangular hole in the ambient temperature plate, and is "back-lit" by the controlled thermal blackbody source. The target ΔT is the temperature difference, in Kelvin or Degrees Celsius, between the blackbody and the target mask. As a detector is scanned across the target, a voltage response is obtained as shown in Figure 8.1(c). This scan line can be either video output, a single detector output, or a gray level if the voltage is acquired with a digital acquisition system. The gain of the FLIR is set to the desired value, usually maximum (NETD can be a function of gain) and if the system has an automatic gain control (AGC), that is disabled. Then, the target-to-background temperature may be optimized (remaining in a linear operating region) to give a signal-to-noise ratio of at least 10 before the measurement.

Once a scan line is obtained, the slope of the system intensity transfer function (SITF) at small differential temperatures is measured. The SITF slope for the scan shown in Figure 8.1(c) is $\Delta S / \Delta T$ where ΔT is the target-to-background differential temperature and ΔS is the measured voltage response. The standard way to measure the voltage response is at the edge — in this case from the background level to the first peak in the scan direction. The rms noise,

N_{rms}, of the background signal is measured on the same line as the target signal voltage response. The NETD is then

$$NETD = \frac{N_{rms}[\text{Volts}]}{\Delta S / \Delta T [\text{Volts}/K]} \tag{8.1}$$

NETD = $\frac{U_{rms}}{\Delta S} \cdot \Delta T$

If $N_{rms} = \Delta S$ ⇒ NETD = ΔT

where the NETD is given in Kelvin. This is a single-point NETD measurement. The shift caused by the ambient temperature and target emissivity offset is a source of systematic error that is avoided by using the SITF slope rather than a single temperature measurement. Another possible error to avoid is heating of the target mask by the blackbody source. The back side of the mask should be reflective, while the front side is highly emissive. The full SITF characterization is shown in Figure 8.1(d). The value used in Equation 8.1 is the slope of the SITF curve at small values of ΔT. In noisy, first generation FLIRs, the temperature difference (for a two-point slope measurement) would be large enough to overcome the noise, but small enough to avoid saturation.

The procedure described above gives a single line NETD. In order to characterize an imaging system, a representative set of lines is used. Also, it is important to ensure that the ambient background temperature in the laboratory is not dramatically different than 300K when measuring systems. A 1 Kelvin differential temperature with a 300K background does not give the same differential radiance as a 1 Kelvin differential temperature with a 280K background. Since the effective ΔT (radiometrically calculated) depends on the ambient background temperature, testing should not be done in an extremely cold or hot environment without radiometric compensation.

8.1.2 Resolution (classical)

The MTF is a measure of system resolution, or the resolution of one of the system components. The modulation transfer function is the modulus of the Optical Transfer Function normalized to unity at a spatial frequency of zero. We normally ignore the "DC" zero frequency term. Theoretically, MTF is the system magnitude response to a set of input sinusoids of various spatial frequencies. It is possible to manufacture sinusoidal target patterns for use in the infrared, but a set for MTF use might be prohibitively expensive. Contrast Transfer Function (CTF) "square wave" targets can be more easily made. The CTF can be measured and then the MTF can be calculated from it. However, the direct methods are not normally used. Methods based on Fourier analysis are the most common.

A typical MTF measurement is shown in Figure 8.2. An MTF target is placed in the focal plane of a collimator as shown in Figure 8.2(a). The target for the 2-D MTF is a circular aperture, while the target for the l-D MTF can be a slit or edge target as shown in Figure 8.2(b). A rule of thumb is that the 2-D MTF target diameter should be less than $1/5^{th}$ of the sensor-under-test detector angular subtense. This limitation restricts the amount of thermal energy through the

pinhole?

pinhole aperture, so a high temperature source must be used. For a linear shift-invariant system, the image of the point source target is the impulse response, or the point spread function *psf(x,y)*, of the system. This does not strictly apply for undersampled systems. An easier option is to measure the l-D MTF by using a line target or an edge target. The response to a line target is called the line spread function, *lsf*. The Fourier transform of the *lsf* is equal to the l-D MTF. This is not equivalent to a "slice" out of the 2-D MTF. The use of an edge target can help in at least two ways: more signal response is obtained and the target size is not an issue as it is for the slit method.

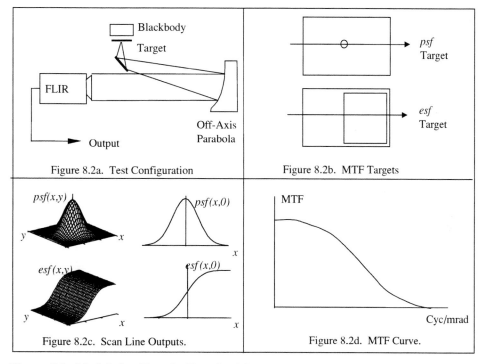

Figure 8.2a. Test Configuration

Figure 8.2b. MTF Targets

Figure 8.2c. Scan Line Outputs.

Figure 8.2d. MTF Curve.

Figure 8.2   Modulation Transfer Function Measurement.

The edge spread function *esf(x,y)* is the response of the imaging system to the edge target. The *esf* is related to the *lsf* in the direction normal to the edge by

$$lsf(x, y) = \frac{d[esf(x, y)]}{dx}.$$

(8.2)

Unlike the *psf*, the *esf* must be measured in both the horizontal and vertical directions to obtain the horizontal and vertical MTF curves. Note that separability is assumed for the edge spread function (see Chapter 2 for the assumption of separability).

Since a slit (impulse function) or an edge (step function) contains all spatial frequencies, the input spectrum of the source is uniform over the sensor

$\mathcal{F}[psf] \Rightarrow MTF \qquad psf = |h|^2$

bandwidth. The two-dimensional Fourier transform of the *psf* gives the MTF of the system. Usually, the spatial axis of the *psf* is in milliradians and the Fourier transform gives a frequency domain function with units of cycles per milliradian.

The 2-D *psf* or the 1-D *esf* or *lsf* can be measured at the output of the detector electronics or with a photometer at the output of the display. The *psf* is a cascade of all system component impulse responses:

$$psf(x, y) = h_{optics}(x, y) ** h_{detector}(x, y) ** h_{electronics}(x, y) ** h_{display}(x, y) ** \dots. \qquad (8.3)$$

The measured system response includes only the component contributions injected up to the measurement point (** denotes two-dimensional convolution). Therefore, the MTF only describes the transfer function of these components:

$$MTF(\xi, \eta) = H_{optics}(\xi, \eta) H_{detector}(\xi, \eta) H_{electronics}(\xi, \eta) H_{display}(\xi, \eta) \dots. \qquad (8.4)$$

This is an important concept since the display can be the limiting component of the system. The eye impulse response, while included in performance models, is not included in the overall system MTF measurement. This brings us to the MRTD, where the human eye-brain response *is* included in the measurement.

8.1.3 Human performance - minimum resolvable temperature difference

The ultimate measure of thermal imaging system performance is a measure of visual acuity of a human observer through the sensor under test. The measurement is called the Minimum Resolvable Temperature Difference (MRTD or just MRT). MRT is a measure of an observer's ability to resolve a four-bar pattern through a sensor under test. Since results depend on observers' training, motivation, and visual acuity, several trained observers are required.

Figure 8.3(a) shows the test configuration with an observer viewing the target image on a display. For characterizing a particular system, the most accurate results are obtained if the display is the actual display to be used with the system in the field, but for comparing systems it may be advantageous to use the same high quality display monitor. A 7:1 aspect ratio 4-bar target is positioned with the bars oriented in the vertical direction in order to measure the horizontal MRT. The azimuth and elevation of the system under test is generally adjusted to center the target in the field of view. The observer is allowed to adjust the monitor and system level and gain during the test. A negative contrast (the bars are cooler than the background) sub-MRT temperature differential is obtained first. The differential temperature is slowly decreased until the observer can resolve all 4 bars. Then, the temperature difference is recorded at which the observer can resolve all 4 bars in positive contrast, again detecting all four bars.

The absolute value of the two measurements are averaged and taken as the MRT for the observer at the spatial frequency of the target. Note that the ambient temperature/emissivity offset is the value in between those two temperature values. The same procedure is performed for all spatial frequency targets.

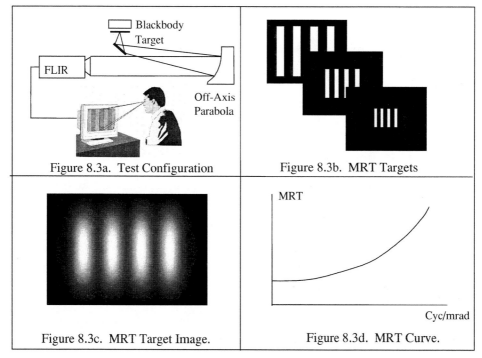

Figure 8.3 Minimum Resolvable Temperature Measurement.

Usually, there are 5 to 8 different targets in the set. Each observer completes up to 3 runs (if the first 2 are not consistent) and averages the MRTD values for each of the spatial frequencies in the target set. Then, the MRTD values for all the observers are averaged together resulting in one curve. This is repeated for both horizontal and vertical bar orientations. The 2-D MRTD curve is calculated from a geometrical average of spatial frequencies corresponding to particular temperature values from the HMRT and VMRT curves. The final measurement is shown in Figure 8.3(d).

Figure 8.4 shows a target wheel with a large number of target selections. This particular wheel is so large and heavy that a crane is needed to move the wheel into position. Figure 8.5 shows a target wheel positioned at the focal plane of an off-axis paraboloid. A fold mirror is used to position the target wheel at the focal plane. Figure 8.6 shows a fixture for positioning cameras to where the targets are in various positions of the field-of-view. Finally, Figure 8.7 shows an engineer performing MRT testing.

8.2 SAMPLED INFRARED IMAGER PERFORMANCE MEASUREMENTS

The classical methods have been extended to address the characteristics associated with sampled imaging systems. We present these new methods in the same general categories as the classical measurement procedures: sensitivity, resolution, and human performance.

Figure 8.4 Target wheel.

Figure 8.5 Target wheel at focal plane of collimator.

Figure 8.6 Camera fixture for target positioning.

Figure 8.7 Engineer performing MRT.

[handwritten annotations at top of page:
x y z
D_x — remove fluct. in x
$1 - D_x$ — remove fluct. in y and z
and yz]

8.2.1 Sensitivity

With the development of advanced focal plane arrays, a single-valued NETD could no longer characterize the noise of sampled imaging systems in an adequate manner. First, as systems became more complex, the reference filter could no longer be applied to accurately limit the bandwidth of the system. The first order filter nature of the filter would not allow the characterization of the complex noise processes of the system. Second, the non-uniformities of the detector arrays contributed significantly to the overall noise of the system. Neither of these noise parameters are represented in the classical NETD measurement. In 1989 and 1990, the U.S. Army Night Vision and Electronic Sensor Directorate (NVESD) developed the three-dimensional noise (3-D Noise) technique along with a laboratory procedure to address these problems.

The concept of directional averaging allows the characterization of complex noise patterns. Consider the 3-D Noise coordinate system shown in Figure 8.8. The 3-D Noise method applies directional averages at the system output port to result in 8 noise components. These components are described in Table 8.1. Note that the subscripts of the noise components indicate the dimensions in which the noise components fluctuate. The parameter σ_{tvh} is most like NETD with the exception that the system bandwidth (not the reference filter bandwidth) determines the spatio-temporal noise value.

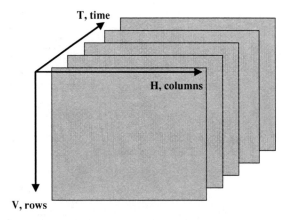

Figure 8.8 3-D Noise coordinate system.

Given three-dimensional image data represented by $U(t,v,h)$, the directional averaging operators are defined as

$$D_t\{U(t,[v],[h])\} = \frac{1}{T}\sum_{t=0}^{T-1} U(t,[v],[h]) \tag{8.5}$$

$$D_v\{U([t],v,[h])\} = \frac{1}{V}\sum_{v=0}^{V-1} U([t],v,[h]) \tag{8.6}$$

$$D_h\{U([t],[v],h)\} = \frac{1}{H}\sum_{h=0}^{H-1} U([t],[v],h) \tag{8.7}$$

where the directional averages are given in Table 8.1. For example, D_v averages each column of pixels in the vertical direction and V is the number of vertical pixels. Each operator collapses the data set in dimension by 1. The operator has an effect of deleting the particular data type from the analysis. The 1-D_t, 1-D_h, 1-D_v operators have the opposite effect. They remove all components that do not have a fluctuation in the desired direction.

The measurement of 3-D Noise involves a target of the same type as used for NETD that is at least 10 times the detector angular subtense of the sensor under test. It is placed just to the left or right of a Region of Interest (ROI) which is used to collect noise data. The ROI is a large uniform background where the noise measurements are obtained. The slope of the SITF of the system is determined in gray levels per degree Celsius in a manner similar to that described in the NETD section. Afterwards, a series of ROI frames are collected for the calculation of 3-D Noise. Note that the reference filter is not used and that the system performance is limited by the system bandwidth, assuming the frame acquisition system does not limit the bandwidth.

Table 8.1. 3-D Noise components

Noise	Component	Potential Source	Directional Operator
σ_{tvh}	Random spatio-temporal noise	Detector temporal noise	$(1\text{-}D_t)(1\text{-}D_v)(1\text{-}D_h)$
σ_{tv}	Temporal row bounce	Line processing, $1/f$, readout	$(1\text{-}D_t)(1\text{-}D_v)D_h$
σ_{th}	Temporal column bounce	Scan effects	$(1\text{-}D_t)D_v(1\text{-}D_h)$
σ_{vh}	Random spatial noise	Pixel processing, detector nonuniformity	$D_t(1\text{-}D_v)(1\text{-}D_h)$
σ_v	Fixed row noise	Detector nonuniformity, $1/f$	$D_t(1\text{-}D_v)D_h$
σ_h	Fixed column noise	Detector nonuniformity, scan effects	$D_tD_v(1\text{-}D_h)$
σ_t	Frame to frame noise	Frame processing	$(1\text{-}D_t)D_vD_h$
S	Mean of all components		$D_tD_vD_h$

An example of a 3-D Noise calculation is shown in Figure 8.9. The component σ_{tv} is desired and the process for finding it is shown. The operator D_h and D_t are applied to the ROI cube. The results are noise planes that include the noise components shown. D_v is applied to the plane on the right in order to obtain a time dependence vector. This time-dependence vector is subtracted from each time row in the plane. The result is that the components based on time alone are removed. The D_h operator is applied to the front plane in order to obtain the vertical noise parameter. This vector is subtracted from each column of the last difference frame to yield a frame that only includes the σ_{tv} component. The standard deviation of the values that are left in the plane give an rms gray level that is converted to a temperature with the SITF conversion factor.

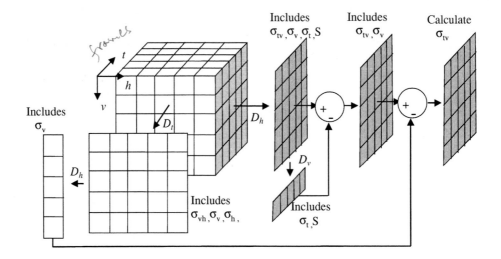

Figure 8.9 3-D Noise example.

Recall that the random spatio-temporal noise, σ_{tvh}, is similar to NETD with the exception that σ_{tvh} is not limited by a reference filter bandwidth (the imager system bandwidth is the limiting bandwidth)

$$\sigma_{tvh} = NETD \frac{\sqrt{\Delta f_s}}{\sqrt{\Delta f_{ref}}}. \tag{8.8}$$

Sometimes σ_{vh}, σ_v, σ_h are given relative to σ_{tvh}. NVESD compiled a database of system noise measurements over a number of years. It was found that for a typical infrared imager, σ_{vh}, σ_{th}, and σ_h are usually negligible. For a scanning system, σ_{tv} is typically $0.25\sigma_{tvh}$, $0.75\sigma_{tvh}$, and $1.0\sigma_{tvh}$, for a low, moderate, and high noise system. Also, σ_v is $0.25\sigma_{tvh}$, $0.75\sigma_{tvh}$, and $1.0\sigma_{tvh}$, respectively. These values are based on circa 1990 and have been reduced in the last few years to give an overall noise estimate a factor of 2 lower. In contrast, the only significant parameter for staring arrays is σ_{vh} at $0.4\sigma_{tvh}$.

3-D Noise is not the only method for characterizing fixed pattern noise in focal plane array imagers. Inhomogeneity Equivalent Temperature Difference (IETD) is defined as the blackbody temperature difference that produces a signal equal to a signal caused by the different responses of the detectors. It is important in staring arrays because it can be the main source of noise. In terms of 3-D Noise, IETD is the collective noise attributed to σ_{vh}, σ_v, σ_h and can be obtained by simply applying the D_t operator.

$$IETD = \sqrt{\sigma_{vh}^2 + \sigma_v^2 + \sigma_h^2}. \tag{8.9}$$

Note that IETD is small when non-uniformity correction has been applied to the sensor under test.

Finally, *correctability* describes the residual spatial noise after the calibration and non-uniformity correction of the sensor and is normalized to the random spatio-temporal noise, σ_{tvh}. A value of "one" means that the spatial noise after correction is equal to the random spatio-temporal noise of the system.

$$C = \frac{\sqrt{\sigma_{vh}^2 + \sigma_v^2 + \sigma_h^2}}{\sigma_{tvh}}. \tag{8.10}$$

The most desirable situation occurs when the sensor is limited by the random spatio-temporal noise (i.e., the correctability is less than one).

8.2.2 Resolution - modulation transfer function (sampled)

Since the MTF target is a point, line, or edge, an undersampled imaging system does not give a shift-invariant response to these targets. A few samples across the target image do not give a good representation of the system response to these inputs. Also, the MTF of a sampled imaging system is not usually measured through the entire system to include the display. The MTF is usually measured using the sampled output of the sensor. Since the system samples only a few points across the optics or detector blur function, the result is a poor representation of the pre-sample MTF. A better measurement is obtained by using the moving slit or the tilted edge method.

The moving slit line spread function method is described in Figure 8.10. The *lsf* is acquired by a series of horizontal movements of a vertically oriented slit. The slit image data are averaged (e.g., 5 times) for each step of the slit. The oversampling rate (the step size compared to the detector pitch or distance in milliradians between samples) is chosen to be around 20. Measurement of the moving slit *lsf* provides a highly sampled *lsf* as shown in Figure 8.10. The measurement is performed on the output of a single pixel as the *lsf* traverses the detector. The measurement can be performed on a number of pixels to verify or increase the precision of the *lsf*.

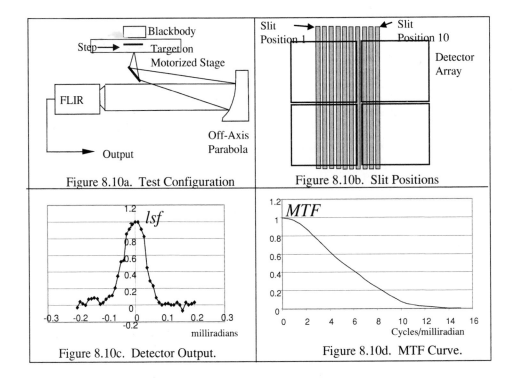

Figure 8.10 Scanning slit MTF method.

The second method for measuring the pre-sample MTF of a sampled imaging system is the super-resolution edge spread function or tilted slit. Consider the method described by Figure 8.11. A knife edge is tilted with respect to the sensor sampling grid. The slope of the knife edge describes the super-resolution oversampling rate. For example, if the knife edge traverses 1 horizontal sample for every 10 vertical samples, the oversampling ratio is 10. For this case, 10 rows of detector outputs are taken across the entire knife edge and interlaced as shown to give a super-resolution rendition of the pre-sample edge spread function. The *esf* is differentiated to give the *lsf* and the Fourier transform is taken in order to yield the MTF.

Since samples are taken to create an accurate rendition of the spatial blur, the MTFs that are measured in the above two procedures only describe a rendition of the pre-sample system MTF. This MTF, in sample space, is actually replicated in frequency. This function does not describe the system post-sample MTF including the display and the eye. However, the measured pre-sample MTF can be used along with a measured or estimated post-sample MTF for two purposes: to determine the baseband transfer function and to determine the spurious response of the system.

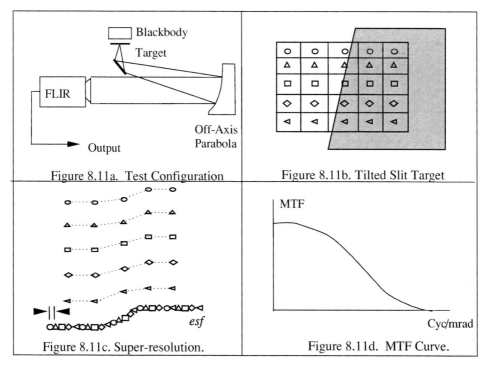

Figure 8.11a. Test Configuration

Figure 8.11b. Tilted Slit Target

Figure 8.11c. Super-resolution.

Figure 8.11d. MTF Curve.

Figure 8.11 Super-resolution edge spread function.

8.2.3 Human performance - minimum resolvable temperature difference

The characteristics of sampled imaging systems have been a serious issue with MRT measurements. With static MRT, a phenomenon occurs between 0.6 and 0.9 times the half-sample (Nyquist) frequency of the sensor. In this region, the transfer response for sampled imaging systems can be degraded significantly or even enhanced. Also, depending on the subjective criteria adopted by a given test facility, the MRT can be measured beyond the half-sample rate of the sensor under test.

Figure 8.12 shows the static approach to measuring MRT of a staring sensor. At each frequency or bar pattern, the phase is found which optimizes the MRT. To vary the phase, the target wheel is placed on a translating stage, or, equivalently, the sensor is placed on a motorized rotational stage. The phase is considered the angular target position with respect to the sensor detector. While the observer views the 4-bar target, the stage is adjusted (i.e., the phase is varied) or the sensor is micro-positioned to peak up the 4-bar target modulation. Between 0.6 and 0.9 times the half-sample rate of the sensor, it is extremely difficult to ensure that correct target phase is accomplished. The results vary greatly with phase and from observer to observer. Figure 8.12(b) shows two images of a 4-bar target where one target is positioned at best phase and the other target is positioned at worst phase. Figure 8.12(c) shows the MRT for a sensor at best phase and at worst phase. Also note in the static MRT figure, the MRT is measured past the half-sample rate of the sensor for the best phase case.

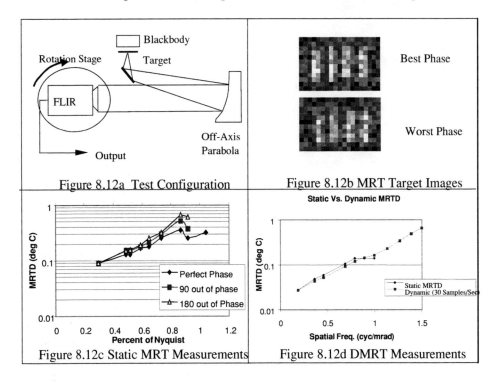

Figure 8.12a Test Configuration

Figure 8.12b MRT Target Images

Figure 8.12c Static MRT Measurements

Figure 8.12d DMRT Measurements

Figure 8.12   Sample imaging system MRT measurements.

In order to address the phase and sampling problems associated with the MRT measurement, Webb developed the dynamic MRT measurement where the MRT target is moved across the sensor field-of-view during the MRT measurement. The technique is known as the Dynamic MRT (DMRT) and the MRT is measured as the target is moved through the sensor's field-of-view. It has been shown that the DMRT can measure system performance up to the MTF limit of the system and eliminate the problems associated with static sampling and phase optimization. The increase in MRT performance is measured due to an increase in the sample rate across the target (as the target moves across the sampling grid). There are two characteristics here worth mentioning. First, while the sampling effect has been minimized in the DMRT measurement, there has been an additional MTF blur introduced by the motion of the target. The DMRT measurement changes with target velocity through the sensor field-of-view since both the spatial sampling rate and the blur due to motion have changed. The DMRT measurement beyond the half-sample rate of the sensor is useful and can be modified for use in acquisition calculations. Webb and Halford describe the DMRT method in detail (see bibliography).

There is a great deal of work that is yet to be performed in the laboratory measurement of sampled imaging systems. The international community is working on many issues associated with the performance measurement of sampled imaging systems. Until these issues are addressed, engineers and acquisition professionals should be cautious of laboratory results and claims of performance with sampled imaging systems. The interpretation of these measurements is taken many different ways and will continue to be taken different ways until a common approach is established.

BIBLIOGRAPHY

Bell, P., C. Hoover, and S. Pruchnic, "Standard NETD test procedure for FLIR systems with video outputs," SPIE Proc., 1969, 194-205, 1993.

Bijl, P. and J. Valeton, "Triangular orientation discrimination: the alternative to minimum resolvable temperature difference and minimum resolvable contrast," Opt. Eng., 37(7), 1976-1983, 1998.

Boreman, G., *Handbook of Optics - Chapter 32 Transfer Function Techniques*, p. 32.8, McGraw-Hill, NY, 1995.

Burroughs, E., R. Driggers, C. Halford, and M. Manzardo, "Beyond MRT," SPIE Proc., 3063, 214-222, 1996.

D'Agostino, J., "Three dimensional noise analysis framework and measurement methodology for imaging system noise," SPIE Proc., 1488, 110-121, 1991.

Driggers, R., C. Halford, G. Boreman, and M. Wellfare, "Comparison of two frame noise calculations for infrared line scanners," Opt. Eng., 27(7), 781-785, 1990.

Driggers, R., G. Boyleston, and G. Edwards, "Equivalent temperature differences with respect to ambient temperature difference as a function of background temperature," Opt. Eng., 31(6), 1357-1361, 1992.

Gaskill, J., *Linear Systems, Fourier Transforms, and Optics*, pp. 343-345, Wiley, NY, 1978.

Holst, G., *The Infrared and Electro-Optical Systems Handbook - Volume 4 Infrared Systems Testing*, p. 235, SPIE and ERIM, 1993.

Hoover, C. and C. Webb, "What is an MRT and how do I get one?," SPIE Proc., 1488, 280-288, 1991.

Hoover, C. and C. Webb, "What is an MRT and how do I get one?," SPIE Proc., 1488, 280-288, 1991.

Lloyd, J.M., *Thermal Imaging Systems,* pp. 166-167, Plenum Press, NY, 1975.

Park, S., R. Schowengerdt, and M. Kaczynski, "Modulation transfer function analysis for sampled imaging systems," Applied Optics, 23(15), 2572-2582, 1984.

Pinson, L., *Electro-Optics*, p. 119, Wiley, NY, 1985.

Pruchnic, S., "Measurements of optical transfer function of discretely sampled thermal imaging systems," SPIE Proc., 1689, 368-378, 1992.

Standard NATO Agreement 4349, *Measurement of the Minimum Resolvable Temperature Difference (MRTD) of Thermal Cameras*, Feb 1994.

Vollmerhausen, R., R. Driggers, and B. O'Kane, "The influence of sampling on target recognition and identification," Opt. Eng., 38(5), 1999.

Vollmerhausen, R., R. Driggers, C. Webb, and T. Edwards, "Staring imager minimum resolvable temperature (MRT) measurements beyond the sensor half sample rate," Opt. Eng., 37(6), 1763-1769, 1998.

Webb, C. and C. Halford, "Dynamic minimum resolvable temperature difference for staring array imagers," Opt. Eng., 38(5), 1999.

Webb, C. and G. Holst, "Observer variables in MRTD," SPIE Proc., 1689, 356-367, 1992.

Webb, C., "Approach to 3-D noise spectral analysis," SPIE Proc., 2470, 288-299, 1995.

Webb, C., "Dynamic minimum resolvable temperature difference for staring focal plane arrays," IRIS Passive Sensors Conference, Johns-Hopkins, March, 1993.

Webb, C., "MRTD, how far can we stretch it?," SPIE Proc., 2224, 294-304, 1994.

Webb, C., "Results of laboratory evaluation of staring arrays," SPIE Proc., 1309, 271-278, 1990.

Webb, C., P. Bell, and G. Mayott, "Laboratory procedures for the characterization of 3-D noise in thermal imaging systems," Proceedings of the IRIS Passive Sensors Symposium, 1991.

Wittenstein, W., "The minimum temperature difference perceived - a new approach to assess undersampled thermal imagers," Opt. Eng., 38(5), 1999.

Wittenstein, W., W. Pick, and W. Raidt, "Simulation study on fixed pattern noise and MRTD," SPIE Proc., 2552, 489-501, 1995.

Wolfe, W. and G. Zissis, *The Infrared Handbook*, pp. 8-31, ERIM, Ann Arbor, MI, 1985.

APPENDIX A
FOURIER SERIES AND FOURIER INTEGRALS

A.1 FOURIER SERIES

This section discusses the harmonic analysis of signals and defines the Discrete Fourier Transform (DFT). For reasons which are given below, neither Fourier series nor the DFT are used when analyzing sampled EO imagers. However, the discussion in this section provides background for the Fourier integral theory described in the next section.

Harmonic analysis consists of projecting the observed signal $f(t)$ onto a basis set of orthogonal sine and cosine functions. That is, a series of N sine and cosine functions is used to represent the observed signal. Assume that t is time, and the signal is observed for T seconds. Then the sines and cosines with periods equal to an integer sub-multiple of T seconds form the orthogonal basis set.

$$f(t) \approx \sum_{k=0}^{N} \left[a_k \cos\left(\frac{2\pi}{T} kt \right) + b_k \sin\left(\frac{2\pi}{T} kt \right) \right] . \tag{A.1}$$

The series in Equation A.1 is periodic with period T. In most practical cases, $f(t)$ is not periodic. Equation A.1 gives the Fourier series for the infinitely repeated $f(t)$. See Figure A.1 for an illustration of this process. The finite, non-periodic function $f(t)$ is made into a periodic function by replicating copies of itself.

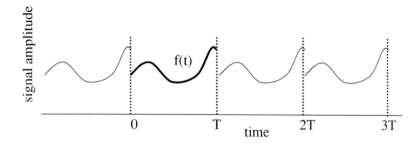

Figure A.1 The function $f(t)$ is replicated to form an infinitely extended, periodic function. The periodic extension of $f(t)$ often has discontinuities at the boundary between replicas.

The a_k and b_k coefficients are found by evaluating the following integrals.

$$a_k = \frac{2}{T} \int_0^T f(t) \cos(\frac{2\pi}{T} kt) \, dt, \ k = 0, \ 1, \ 2, \ 3, \ldots$$

$$b_k = \frac{2}{T} \int_0^T f(t) \sin(\frac{2\pi}{T} kt) \, dt, \ k = 1, \ 2, \ 3, \ldots \quad (A.2)$$

Equations A.1 and A.2 can be cast in an exponential form which more resembles the Fourier transforms found in this book. The series is:

$$f(t) \approx \sum_{k=-N/2}^{N/2} \alpha_k e^{j2\pi \, kt/T} \quad (A.3)$$

where

$$\alpha_k = \frac{1}{T} \int_{-T/2}^{T/2} f(t) e^{-j2\pi \, kt/T} \, dt \quad for \ k = 0, \ \pm 1, \ \pm 2, \ \pm 3, \ldots \quad (A.4)$$

and the α_k are complex numbers.

The Fourier series is a representation or approximation to the function $f(t)$ in the interval $0 \le t \ge T$. In the frequency domain, each k/T corresponds to a discrete frequency. The function $f(t)$ is made periodic and then decomposed into a set of sinusoidal waves. Equations A.1 and A.3 give the Fourier series for the infinitely repeated function.

Trigonometric functions are unique in that uniformly spaced samples over an integer number of periods form an orthogonal basis set. In the above equations, $f(t)$ can be sampled, and the integrals can be turned into sums. Assume that N samples are taken in time T. Then:

$$a_k = \sum_{n=0}^{N-1} f(\frac{nT}{N}) \cos(2\pi \ knT/N) \ for \ k = 0, \ 1, \ 2, \ .., N/2$$

$$b_k = \sum_{n=0}^{N-1} f(\frac{nT}{N}) \sin(2\pi \ knT/N) \ for \ k = 0, \ 1, \ 2, \ .., N/2. \quad (A.5)$$

The representation of $f(t)$ is now:

$$f(t) \approx \sum_{k=0}^{N/2} \left[a_k \cos\left(\frac{2\pi}{T} kt \right) + b_k \sin\left(\frac{2\pi}{T} kt \right) \right]. \quad (A.6)$$

It should be noted that the Equation A.6 approximation for $f(t)$ is not the same as the Equation A.1 approximation. In Equation A.6, the a_k and b_k are found from the sampled values of $f(t)$.

Equations A.2, A.4, and A.5 represent discrete line spectra, because the a_k, b_k, and α_k are amplitudes of sinusoidal waves. However, Equations A.1, A.3, and A.6 are continuous representations of $f(t)$. It is often convenient to have discrete versions of both the frequency domain and space or time domain functions. One might assume that the samples of $f(t)$ [the $f(nT/N)$ samples in Equation A.5] can represent the function in time (space). However, in that case, the time (space) representations do not have an inverse Fourier relationship to the discrete frequency components. Remember that the series representation of $f(t)$ is only an approximation.

However, the discrete time samples which result from sampling Equation A.6 have the correct relationship to the discrete frequency spectra in Equation A.5. Equations A.5 and A.7 form a discrete transform pair. That is, substituting $f'(nT/N)$ from Equation A.7 into Equation A.5 yields the a_k and b_k which, when substituted into Equation A.7, yields the $f'(nT/N)$ values.

$$ f'(\frac{nT}{N}) = \sum_{k=0}^{N/2} \left[a_k \cos\left(\frac{2\pi}{N} kn \right) + b_k \sin\left(\frac{2\pi}{N} kn \right) \right] \ for \ n = 0, 1, \ldots, N-1 . $$

(A.7)

The fidelity with which the Fourier series in Equations A.1, A.3, A.6, or A.7 represents $f(t)$ depends on many factors. Certainly k must be large enough to span the frequency content in $f(t)$. Too few terms in the series leads to errors in the approximation. Also, the Gibb's phenomenon will lead to considerable error in the region of any discontinuity in $f(t)$. Remember that $f(t)$ is made into a periodic function by replicating copies of itself. As illustrated in Figure A.1, there is normally a discontinuity at the border between replicas of $f(t)$. Other errors arise because the Fourier series only represents a finite number of frequencies. Frequencies in $f(t)$ not represented in the series will either "leak" and appear as a wrong frequency component or will not be included in the series representation.

Also, although the discrete transform defined by Equations A.5 and A.7 is widely used with sampled data, neither the DFT nor the Fourier series provide insight into the sampling characteristics of the system. The DFT depends on the sample values and does not express the Fourier transform of a sampled version of $f(t)$ in terms of the pre-sample MTF, the sample rate, and the post-sample MTF.

The Fourier integral transform provides a more accurate representation of a non-periodic signal than does the Fourier series. Also, the integral transform provides the flexibility to express the Fourier transform of a sampled $f(t)$ in terms of the pre- and post-sample MTFs and sample rate.

A.2 FOURIER INTEGRAL

Equations A.3 and A.4 are generalized to allow any frequency and to permit $f(t)$ to be non-periodic. The sums become integrals, and the $-T/2 \le t \ge T/2$ interval now extends over all time.

$$F(\xi) = \int_{-\infty}^{\infty} f(t)e^{-j2\pi\xi t}dt \tag{A.8}$$

$$f(t) = \int_{-\infty}^{\infty} F(\xi)e^{j2\pi\xi t}df. \tag{A.9}$$

Equations A.8 and A.9 define the Fourier integral transform pair, where ξ is frequency in Hertz. If t represents angle in milliradians rather than time, then ξ is frequency in cycles per milliradian. If t represents a spatial coordinate in units of millimeters, then ξ is frequency in cycles per millimeter.

The condition for existence of $F(\xi)$ is generally given as:

$$\int_{-\infty}^{\infty} |f(t)|dt < \infty \tag{A.10}$$

or, in other words, $f(t)$ must be absolutely integrable. However, Equation A.10 is sufficient but not necessary; $f(t)$ often exists even if this condition is not met.

Three properties of the Fourier transform are used often in this book. The first property is linearity. If $F(\xi)$ is the Fourier transform of $f(t)$, and $G(\xi)$ is the Fourier transform of $g(t)$, then the Fourier transform of $[f(t) + g(t)]$ is $[F(\xi) + G(\xi)]$. The second property is time-shifting. If $F(\xi)$ is the Fourier transform of $f(t)$, then the Fourier transform of $f(t-\tau)$ is $F(\xi)e^{-j2\pi\xi\tau}$.

The third property is that if $f(x,y)$ is separable, then the Fourier transform of $f(x,y)$ is separable. That is, if:

$$f(x,y) = g(x)h(y), \tag{A.11}$$

then

$$F(\xi,\eta) = G(\xi)H(\eta). \tag{A.12}$$

Another theorem used throughout the book is that a convolution in the space domain is a multiplication in the frequency domain. That is:

$$\text{If } h(t) = \int_{-\infty}^{\infty} f(\tau)g(\tau-t)d\tau \tag{A.13}$$

$$\text{then } H(\xi) = F(\xi)G(\xi).$$

An asterisk is used in this book to represent convolution. For example, $h(t) = f(t) * g(t)$.

Some Fourier transform pairs are shown in the figures below. The symbol $\Leftrightarrow$ indicates the transform pair relationship. In Figure A.2, the transform of a rect function is a sinc function. In Figure A.3, the transform of a constant is a delta function. In Figure A.4, the transform of a Gaussian is a Gaussian.

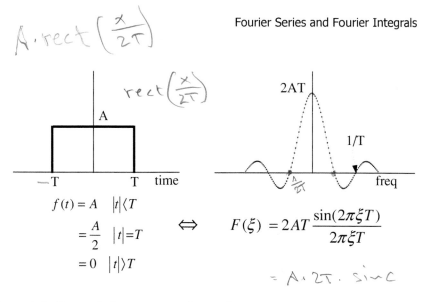

$A \cdot rect\left(\frac{x}{2T}\right)$

$rect\left(\frac{x}{2T}\right)$

$f(t) = A \quad |t| \langle T$

$\qquad = \dfrac{A}{2} \quad |t| = T$

$\qquad = 0 \quad |t| \rangle T$

$\Leftrightarrow \quad F(\xi) = 2AT \dfrac{\sin(2\pi\xi T)}{2\pi\xi T}$

$= A \cdot 2T \cdot sinc$

Figure A.2 Rect and sinc wave transform pair.

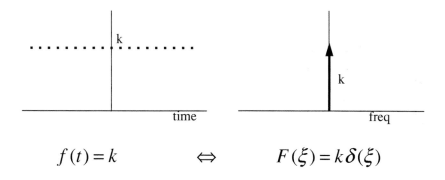

$$f(t) = k \qquad \Leftrightarrow \qquad F(\xi) = k\delta(\xi)$$

Figure A.3 The transform of a constant is a delta function centered at the frequency origin.

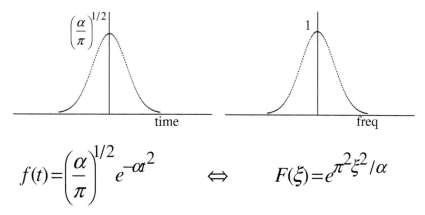

$$f(t) = \left(\frac{\alpha}{\pi}\right)^{1/2} e^{-\alpha t^2} \qquad \Leftrightarrow \qquad F(\xi) = e^{\pi^2 \xi^2 / \alpha}$$

Figure A.4 The transform of a Gaussian is a Gaussian.

APPENDIX B
THE IMPULSE FUNCTION

B.1 DEFINITION

The impulse function is also known as the Dirac delta function. It can be described as a function that has an infinite height, zero width and an area equal to unity. Mathematically, the impulse function is defined by Equation B.1.

$$\int_{-\infty}^{\infty} \delta(x - x_0) f(x) dx = f(x_0).$$ (B.1)

For practical purposes, we can define $\delta(x)$ as follows.

$$\delta(x) = \lim_{b \to 0} \frac{1}{|b|} Gauss(\frac{x}{b}).$$ (B.2)

The area under the Gaussian function must remain unity as b gets smaller, so the height of the function increases as shown in Figure B.1. The practical definition given in Equation B.2 could have used the rectangle or a number of other shapes. The important concept is that the impulse function has zero width but unity area.

B.2 PROPERTIES OF THE IMPULSE FUNCTION

There are a few important properties of the impulse response that are used frequently throughout this text. One of the defining properties of the impulse function is

$$\delta(x - x_o) = 0, \; x \neq x_o$$ (B.3)

so that the only location where the impulse function has a non-zero value is at the location of the impulse function. Another defining property is the integral property of the impulse function

$$\int_{-\infty}^{\infty} \delta(x - x_o) dx = 1$$ (B.4)

which simply states that the area of an impulse function is 1. The *sifting* property is described as such because the impulse function "sifts" out the value of a function at a particular point

$$\int_{x_1}^{x_2} f(x)\delta(x-x_o)dx = f(x_o) \qquad x_1 < x_o < x_2.$$ (B.5)

The impulse function is an even function, so that

$$\delta(x) = \delta(-x).$$ (B.6)

The *comb* function is an infinite set of equally spaced delta functions. The *comb* function has been described with many different notations including Bracewell's "shah" function. The Fourier transform of a comb function in space is a comb function in frequency. If X is the spacing between delta functions, then

$$\sum_{n=-\infty}^{\infty} \delta(x-nX) \Leftrightarrow \sum_{n=-\infty}^{\infty} \delta(\xi-n/X)$$ (B.7)

where $\Leftrightarrow$ indicates a Fourier transform pair.

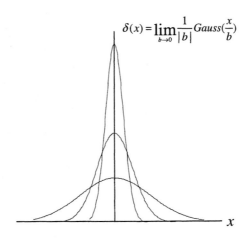

$$\delta(x) = \lim_{b \to 0} \frac{1}{|b|} Gauss(\frac{x}{b})$$

Figure B.1 As the width of the Gaussian decreases, the height increases in order to maintain the area under the curve at unity.

INDEX

Aberrations, 2, 24, 28

Active area of detector (*also see* fill factor), 2-3, 25

Airy disc, 29

Aliasing (*also see* spurious response), 5, 46, 51, 93

Ambient optical flow, 130

Artifacts (*see* sampling artifacts)

Atmosphere, 89

Band-limited function, 13, 141, 143, 145

Bar pattern, 88, 143, 147, 152

Baseband spectrum, 51

Bilinear interpolation, 12, 77-84

Camera, 2

Cartesian coordinates, 28, 46

Cathode ray tube, 37

Causality, 41

Classical design criteria, 85

Comb of delta functions, 50

Constant parameter systems, 11

Contrast transfer function, 150

Convolution kernels, 79-84

Convolution, 24

Correctability, 159

Correlation, 132

CRT raster (*see* raster and cathode ray tube)

Cycles on target, 89-91

Delta function (also see impulse function), 17, 50, 171

Design examples, 96-107

Detection, 88

Detector angular subtense (DAS), 35

Detector array (*also see* focal plane array), 3

Diagonal dither, 117

Diffraction (*see* modulation transfer function—diffraction)

Direction averagers, 156

Discrete Fourier transform (*also see* Fourier series), 127, 165

Discrete interpolation functions, 84

Discrimination tasks (*see* task performance metrics)

Display as a filter, 17

Display filtering (*see* display pixels)

Display MTF (*see* display pixels and modulation transfer function—display)

Display pixel—rectangular, 4, 73, 101

Display pixels—Gaussian, 73

Display pixels: effect of shape and size, 5, 14, 37, 50, 53, 144

Display, 3

Displayed frequency spectrum (*see* display pixels and Fourier transform of sampled image)

Displayed image, 49

Dither mirror, 111, 120

Dither, 111, 125, 130

Dither for static scene, 114

Dynamic MRT, 148, 162

Dynamic sampling, 125, 130

Edge spread function, 151

Effect of changing sample rate, 56

Electronic filtering (see MTF – electronics)

Equivalent Blur, 96

Eye blur (*also see* modulation transfer function—eye), 5

Fidelity, 13, 17
Field, 111
Fill factor, 3
Flat panel displays, 74, 101
Focal plane array (FPA), 2, 14, 25, 111
Fourier domain filtering, 25
Fourier integral transform, 23, 127, 167
Fourier series, 165
Fourier transform of delta function, 18
Fourier transform of sampled function, 14, 17
Fourier transform of sampled image, 17, 18, 21
Fourier transform of samples, 17
Frame, 111

Generalized motion estimation, 134
Geometric image, 136
Gradient estimation, 132

Half-sample limit, 77, 88, 91, 92, 95
Half-sample rate, 145
Hot-spot detection, 94
Human performance (see task performance metrics)

Ideal filters, 139, 145
Identification performance, 88, 89, 94, 107
Image phase, 133
Image reconstruction (*see* reconstruction)
Image restoration, 136
Imaging system performance (*see* task performance metrics)
Impulse function, 23, 41, 52, 171
In-band aliasing, 68, 93, 120
In-band spurious response, 68, 94
In-band spurious response ratio, 68

Inhomogeneity equivalent temperature difference, 147, 159
InSb imager, 121
Integrate and hold circuit, 35
Interlace, 111, 124
Interpolation function, 73-85
Interpolation kernels, 81
Isoplanatic, 24

Johnson criteria, 88-92

Kell factor, 84, 87

Laboratory measurements, 147
Leqault's criterion, 86
Line spread function, 151
Linear interpolation, 12, 79, 84
Linear superposition (*see* superposition)
Linear, 23
Linearity, 7
LSI system, 8, 10, 26

Maximum likelihood, 133
Microscan (see dither)
Microscan mirror, 111
Minimum resolvable contrast, 88
Minimum resolvable temperature difference measurement, 88, 147, 152, 161
Modulation transfer function, 25, 147, 162
Modulation transfer function—detector, 25, 34, 129
Modulation transfer function—diffraction, 2, 28, 32
Modulation transfer function—display, 14, 21, 25, 38, 45, 50, 52, 74, 76
Modulation transfer function—electronics, 36, 40
Modulation transfer function—eye, 38, 52, 74, 76, 101
Modulation transfer function—interpolation, 76, 83

Modulation transfer function—measurement, 150

Modulation transfer function—optics, 32

Modulation transfer function—post-sample, 76

Motion artifacts, 122-123

Motion blur, 35

MTF squeeze, 92, 94

Nodding mirror, 111

Noise equivalent temperature difference measurement, 147, 149

Non-interlace operation, 123

Non-sampled imagers, 45

Non-separable functions, 29, 117

Non-shift invariant, 17, 53

One-dimensional analysis, 28

Optical aberrations (see aberrations)

Optical flow, 125, 134

Optical transfer function (OTF), 7

Optimum sampling, 6, 84

Out-of-band aliasing, 68, 93

Out-of-band spurious response, 68, 73, 84, 94

Out-of-band spurious response ratio, 68

Output spectrum, 20

Parallel scan thermal imagers, 35

Phase correlation, 133

Phase transfer function, 25

Photo-current, 2

Photo-detection, 2

Photo-electron, 2

Pixel replication, 5, 74, 79, 84

Pixelated display, 7

Point spread function (psf), 23, 25, 31, 45, 52, 126, 152

Polar coordinates, 28

Post-sample MTF, or blur, 5, 45

Power spectral density, 136

Pre-sample MTF, or blur, 3, 4, 14, 45, 119

Pseudo-image, 126, 136

Random spatio-temporal noise, 158

Raster, 7, 46, 51, 87, 95

Recognition performance, 88, 94, 107

Reconstructing bar pattern image, 143

Reconstruction, 3, 5, 12-14, 50, 73, 77

Reconstruction function, 13, 14, 17, 78

Reconstruction with sampling theorem, 140

Rect (rectangular) function, 14, 36, 139

Rectangular display element, 37

Replicated spectra, 50-51

Replication (see pixel replication)

Resolution enhancement, 125

Resolution, 119, 147, 150

Resolved cycles (see cycles on target)

Response function, 45, 52

Sample and hold, 8

Sample function, 141

Sample imager performance measurements, 153

Sample interval, 14, 21, 45, 46, 52, 53

Sample phase, 21, 49, 52

Sample point, 49

Sample rate, 13

Sample spacing (see sample interval)

Sampled imager design, 73

Sampled imager optimization, 73, 95

Sampled imager response function, 45, 52, 54

Sampled Imager, 2, 45, 92

Sampled spectrum, 52-56, 74

Samples per IFOV, 36
Sampling artifacts, 6, 45, 50, 51, 52, 92
Sampling limitations, 126
Sampling process, 4, 14, 17, 21, 50
Sampling replicas (see replicated spectra)
Sampling Theorem, 88, 139
Sampling Theorem misconceptions, 139, 143-145
Scanning slit MTF, 160
Scene function, 126
Scene-to-sensor motion, 122
Schade's criterion, 84-86
Sensitivity, 119, 148
Separability, 28, 46, 117
Sequin's criterion, 84, 87-88
Shift estimation, 130
Shift invariance, 7-10, 17, 23
Sinc wave, 13, 140
Slit response, 151
Sombrero function (somb), 29
Spatial domain filtering, 26
Spatial filter, 24
Spatio-temporal noise parameter, 148
Spurious response (*also see* aliasing), 51-53, 73, 82
Spurious response ratio, 68
Spurious response terms, 54
Standard video, 112
Staring array imager, 2, 105
Steady state analysis, 10
Super-resolution edge spread function, 161
Super-resolution, 125
Superposition, 7, 24
System amplitude response, 52
System intensity transfer function, 149
System magnification, 53
System noise, 148
System response function, 7
System transfer function (*see* transfer response)

Task performance metrics, 54, 86-95, 107, 152, 161
Television resolution (*also see* Kell factor), 87
Temporal filters, 40
Three-dimensional noise, 147, 156, 157
Tilted edge spread function, 161
Transfer function (*see* transfer response)
Transfer function of eye (*see* modulation transfer function—eye)
Transfer response, 7, 10, 11, 17, 31, 50, 53, 82, 119
Transfer response of sampled imager, 45
Translation phase term, 20

Undersampled imager, 6, 119, 120
Unity magnification, 23

Video display rates, 112
Video interlace (see interlace)
Video raster (see raster)
Visible display raster (see raster)

Weiner filter spectral response, 137
Weiner restoration filter, 136
Well-corrected optical system, 25
Well-sampled imager, 6, 120

Comments:

1. Why is visible pixelation ≡ out of band spurious content?

 **Mr. Richard H. Vollmerhausen** currently heads the Model Development Branch at the US Army's Night Vision Lab. The branch is updating the Army's target acquisition models to include the effect of sampling on performance and to make other model enhancements in order to predict the performance of advanced technology sensors. During his tenure at NVL, he was a project engineer and EO systems analyst for numerous Army weapon systems. His previous work included designing air-to-air missile seekers for the Navy and working as an Instrumentation Engineer for Douglas Aircraft on the Saturn/Apollo Program. Mr. Vollmerhausen is the author of two books on electro-optical systems analysis and has published numerous journal and symposium papers.

 **Dr. Ronald G. Driggers** has 12 years of electro-optics experience and has worked for or consulted to Lockheed Martin, SAIC, EOIR Measurements, Amtec Corporation, Joint Precision Strike Demonstration Project Office, and Redstone Technical Test Center. He is currently working for the US Army's Night Vision and Electronic Sensors Directorate and is the U.S. representative to the NATO panel on advanced thermal imager characterization. Dr. Driggers is the author of two books on infrared and electro-optics systems and has published over 30 refereed journal papers. He is editor of Marcel Dekker's *Encyclopedia of Optical Engineering* and is an Associate Editor of *Optical Engineering*.